THE CURE FOR MENTAL ILLNESS

THE SOLUTION TO SUICIDE

DAVID WILLIAM JONES

The Cure for Mental Illness: The Solution to Suicide
Written by David William Jones

Copyright © 2024 by David William Jones

All rights reserved.

No part of this publication may be reproduced, distributed or transmitted in any form or by any means, including photocopying, recording, artificial intelligence or other electronic or mechanical methods or otherwise, without the prior written permission of the publisher.

Published by
Light in the Darkness Guidance and Transformation Services

Website:
www.lightinthedarkness.online
QR code:

First edition: 2024
ISBN: 978-1-7636997-2-4
Cover designed by Rebeca Covers
Illustrations by Anastasia Soroka
Edited by David William Jones

TABLE OF CONTENTS

INTRODUCTION 5

CHAPTER 1: MY STORY 9
CHAPTER 2: WHAT'S WRONG WITH THE CURRENT SYSTEM? 21
CHAPTER 3: UNDERSTANDING SUICIDE,
THE CAUSES OF SUICIDE 33
CHAPTER 4: FOR THOSE WHO HAVE LOST 41
CHAPTER 5: FOR THOSE WHO ARE THINKING
AND FEELING SUICIDAL 45
CHAPTER 6: RECOGNIZING YOUR TRUE VALUE 51
CHAPTER 7: THE SOLUTION TO SUICIDE 55
CHAPTER 8: THE SEQUENCE TREE – IDENTITY,
THOUGHTS, EMOTIONS AND ACTIONS. 59
CHAPTER 9: THE SUPERPOWER OF PRESENCE 67
CHAPTER 10: THE STAGE OF LIFE - "ALL THE WORLD'S A STAGE" 77

CHAPTER 11: THE SECRET OF THE WORDS – "I WANT TO KILL MYSELF" — 91

CHAPTER 12: THE POWER OF SELF INQUIRY MEDITATION – "WHO AM I?" — 99

CHAPTER 13: POTENTIAL RESISTANCES AND IMPEDIMENTS TO SELF INQUIRY MEDITATION — 115

CHAPTER 14: THE TRAP OF SELF-ESTEEM AND SELF-WORTH — 119

CHAPTER 15: ENLIGHTENMENT AND TRUE HAPPINESS — 123

FINAL THOUGHTS — 127

INTRODUCTION

In this particular book, as part of this series: The Cure for Mental Illness, I will be focusing on the subject of Suicide, bringing awareness to Humanity about how to internally overcome suicidal thoughts, emotions and behaviours.

I will be sharing with you some completely new and unique ways that I have discovered from my own lived experience. Revealing to you the biggest secrets about solving suicide that no medication can do for you, that no Psychs, Doctors or other so called "professional" supports will tell you. Simply because, for the most part they themselves don't have the lived experience that I have of living through it. Nor do they have the level of experience I have in true awakening to reach full understanding of the mind and reality, to go as deeply inward as I have in order to solve and heal mental illness, suicide and many other challenges that have impacted the lives of many people.

The information that I will be sharing with you, is mostly based on my own direct lived experience through the mental health system of Australia, however the content and solutions that I will be discussing are universal and relevant to all.

As someone with lived experience of Mental illness, being suicidal and knowing what it takes to overcome them both completely, which in and of itself is quite frankly a more significant feat than someone discovering the cure for cancer, because mental illness impacts many more people. With my lived experience, I am more than qualified to provide the necessary navigation for humanity to naturally overcome this challenge to solve Mental Illness and suicide once and for all, providing you with the key understandings which make all the difference.

Suicide has been a somewhat taboo subject that people would have generally wanted to stay away from because it's a matter of life and death, which can have a deeply emotional impact on all involved. Suicide itself is a final and irreversible act of leaving the body, which doesn't just impact our own life, it impacts all of us. It is a loss for all of the human family, because for every life lost, there is a trail of grief and potentially detrimental actions by those affected, grieving the loss of loved ones.

If we are carrying around with us such grievances and pain in our hearts as a result of losing our loved ones to suicide, then depending upon how well we cope with that, it can positively or negatively impact many places and people on our path.

The grieving and broken state of being ripples out to all of humanity, impacting the lives of many.

Some may take the path of turning to detrimental coping mechanisms such as alcohol abuse and other drugs which may present additional challenges and harm to society as a whole.
Other coping mechanisms can result in beneficial individual development and advancement for the entire species, inspiring others to be stronger, to communicate, to address problems and challenges

before they become bigger issues and to have more gratitude for each day and what they have.

For every life lost to suicide, it is a reminder that collectively we haven't got things right.

For someone to get to a point of suffering where they are choosing not to live life on this beautiful planet, is a clear indication of a system and society that is flawed and has clearly failed in its approaches towards prevention, and also towards helping and supporting people who are confronted with such a degree of internal suffering.

This is because the failed system has never taught people how to deal with suicide properly, neither through education systems, nor professionally with clients in mental health settings or otherwise.
The evidence of this is clearly reflected not only in the numerous lived experiences of those of us who have been subject to the heartless and inhumane practices and procedures of the mental health systems, but also, the evidence of a failed system is clearly seen in the resulting statistics of suicide which I will now share with you.

In Australia, as of the year 2024, According to the national suicide prevention office, every day approximately 9 people die by suicide and 150 people attempt to take their own life.

This is approximately 3250 deaths and 54,750 attempts each year.
While Suicide Prevention Australia reports that Male suicides currently make up approximately 75% of all Suicides, with ambulances responding to over 16,800 calls every year from males experiencing suicidal thoughts and with more than 9,000 ambulances responding to suicide attempts.

However, the most alarming statistic, is the fact that the vast majority (well over 50%) of the people who have committed suicide, had previously received mental health support from professionals.

So what does that tell us about how professional, helpful, and effective the mental health systems and their approaches really are? Obviously they are no where near good enough.

Of course, suicide has not only occurred in Australia, it has been a global issue, and suicide is a loss for all of humanity.

These kind of statistics from my own and other's countries all over the world indicate that there is a major failure in this area.
Both for causing people to get to that point in themselves of wanting to take their own lives, and also for not being able to prevent the loss of life.
This reflects the fact that this world and it's systems aren't yet good enough, because the value of life has not been recognised, taught, nor appreciated by the mainstream systems and there are reasons for that which I will also be covering throughout this series.

Although these statistics are alarming to say the least, it's not all dark and grim, for it is by our failures that we have the opportunity to learn and grow to make things right.
So, when it comes to Suicide, the very good news that I have to share with you all, is that Suicide is completely preventable.

From my lived experience of years of suffering and hardships that I endured internally and externally in order to discover The Cure for Mental Illness, I am also pleased to announce that I have also discovered the Solution for Suicidal thoughts emotions and behaviours along the way.

CHAPTER 1:

MY STORY

This is only a small part of my story and who I am that I can share with you at this time. I will be revealing more about who I am in an "about the author" section in an up and coming part of this series

When it comes to my story and experience regarding suicide, I never caused a great deal of physical harm to my own body when I was depressed and feeling suicidal. I had my own ways of coping with it. But coping wasn't enough, I had to do something about it, and when I did, I discovered some unexpected hidden gems to solving it altogether.

To give you some idea of my background experience with this, I must have been somewhere around the age of 14 to 16 years young when I first cut my wrist in front of the teacher, drawing blood with a pair of blunt scissors. I did this mainly to shut the teacher up and stop them from bullying other children with their bossy attitude and rules. Additionally I had my own issues, I hated school and I was overwhelmed by all of the control and corruption that I could see in the education system and everywhere else.

I always had a gift of a very deep perception to see under the surface of things. Through my eyes, I could see that there was so much wrong with the world and humans in general, like I had to fix everything.

For various reasons, the thought of suicide was often on my mind after leaving high school.

How I felt about myself and the world I lived in, just seemed like the life wasn't worth living, the only thing that kept me going was knowing from a younger age that I was here for a higher mission. It seemed that everyone was trained and directed to live a boring life of mediocrity and slavery, blinded to the magic of life and what their reality could be. To go through school wasting their youth, then 3-5 years wasted in University, just to get a boring 9 to 5 hamster wheel job to pay for food and to live somewhere, to then settle down and have kids.
All for the purpose of putting them through the same monotonous and meaningless existence in a fake world, I could see that even the birds in the garden had much more freedom than humans, it was a very depressing thought to say the least.

It seemed absolutely wasteful, pointless and stupid to me to live my life according to that robotic script like most other people.
I couldn't understand how anyone could possibly be truly happy and fulfilled by doing that, and they obviously weren't, their unhappiness was written on their faces.
I decided that's not the life I wanted, I knew there was so much more to who we are, our life and our reality.
However, like many other children, I'd already been forced to waste all that time in school with them putting so much academic pressure on us, in order for us to live that way and be that way, trying to shape us into being a shape we weren't created to be, trying to make us live

by the mainstream procedure towards a mediocre life like everyone else, which in my eyes wasn't life at all.

This is why most often I didn't even try at school, because I knew that school was just a stepping stone to live that shitty existence that they were all planning for us, and as a child, I knew that if they got it all wrong, then why should I follow them?

I knew that they must not realise what else is possible and most important in life, that they must not be able to see what I see, beyond the mundane reality, even most of the adults were baby souls to me despite them always ignorantly thinking that they were the boss just because they were physically older.

There was no mystical nor magical quality to their lives, nor could I see any adult striving beyond the boundaries of their conditioning, to make their life something truly exciting and inspirational. Everywhere I looked, it seemed to be that there was a force intentionally working against humanity's best interests, taking the magic and colour out of life for everyone. After much depression through the years, from being isolated and alone so much at an age when I should have been socialising and out in the world, I had many reasons to feel bad. Over time, the surmounting shit reality and controlled life took it's toll on me.

I started to genuinely contemplate suicide throughout my early to mid 20's. I wasn't where I wanted to be and at that time I felt that there were too many things and people holding me back from making the life that I wanted to live.

Although this was mostly true, I later recognised that I lacked the necessary responsibility and clarity of direction at that time, for how to see beyond the fog of my situation and take the driver seat and wheel of my own life to leave the people who were trying to control and manipulate me to keep me stuck.

I could also see the control and slavery of humanity with all of the brainwashing, I knew this wasn't how humanity was meant to be, that humanity could be so much more. I could see beneath the surface of everything in the fake world and it's manipulative and controlling systems and all of it's ways for deceiving humanity. I told my family about what I saw, but they were all too ignorant to listen to me at the time, which made me very upset and very angry for never being heard.

I experienced a period of time where I was waking up every day only wanting to die. I was about 22 when I tried to drown myself in a bathtub before being pulled out. The thoughts of suicide continued to stir in my mind as a real option, because they had not been dealt with at the root. At the time I didn't know what the root was exactly, nor how to deal with the noise of the mind and those detrimental thoughts of suicide.

Due to it not being dealt with at the root, it grew back in the same way like a weed does if you don't deal with it by pulling it out by the root. It became so severe, to the point where it had become normal for me to be waking up every single day only wanting to die. It wasn't until about 24 to 25 that I decided to finally challenge the relentless voices of depression and suicide that I was living with every single day and night.

So, I decided to jump out of an aeroplane, i.e by going skydiving.
I did this in order to put myself in a situation where survival was completely unknown. By doing so, I would be confronted with the very real possibility that the parachute might not pull and that survival was not guaranteed, until my feet were back on the ground. It was a great

big dive into the unknown for me, but I felt an inner calling to do that, so I did. Once I jumped, my adrenaline went to 100%, the whole body knew that there was a real possibility of death, it was preparing for it. It was during this time that I was internally faced with the existential question that I heard within me: *"Do you want to live?"*.

I screamed *"YES!"* inside me.

When the parachute pulled and came out safely, I felt a great relief. I enjoyed gliding over the land below, and seeing the beautiful landscape surrounding my childhood hometown, where I grew up in my youngest years. I knew at that moment that I definitely wanted to live, because I was clearly grateful for the parachute coming out and I was grateful for my life. I could see so much more value in life than before I had jumped, and so I knew that I made the right choice by doing so.

From then on, I knew that whenever the thoughts of suicide came again, that I would remember that experience. I knew that such thoughts of suicide or self harm were pointless and that I shouldn't waste any more time on them because I'd already confronted them.
After that experience, I knew that I wasn't ever going to actually do it, that I wasn't ever going to kill myself.
The experience of skydiving forced me to decide, and so I knew that I wasn't ready to leave this life and that I wanted to live.
The intense lived experience solidified the memory in me within every cell of my body, to never go back to the drama of feeling and thinking in a suicidal way ever again.

Eventually the voices stopped altogether because I would remind myself and those thoughts if they were to ever come up again, I would tell them: *"we have already been through this and I already know that leaving this life is not an option, I already know that I want to live, so just shut up"*, and so they did.

I came to understand how important our attention is and how important it is to be aware about what people and thoughts consume our attention.
Because the less I gave any attention to any notion of suicide then the less that idea was fed by any of my energy, the less that idea came up, until eventually they were completely gone, because I starved them of my attention and energy and therefore they could not grow.

This is an important mechanism to be aware of for overcoming mental illness, suicidal ideation and it is also important to understand for creating the reality we prefer, this mechanism is simply summarised by the expression
"Energy flows, where attention goes"
So next time you watch television and apply this awareness you will see that the media intentionally wants you to focus your attention on detrimental things that make you feel in fear, worry, wanting you to focus on anxiety invoking subjects, on divisive subjects and subjects that bend opinions to support the narratives of corrupt agendas.

Though let's not get too far off topic, I will be exposing the subject of media corruption and mass manipulation in other subjects of this series because they have played a major role in the deception, detriment and mental illness of humanity.

Continuing now with our subject on the solution to suicide.

From my experience of skydiving, I realised that anyone who is truly feeling suicidal won't be afraid to skydive, because if they are truly considering leaving this life, then they will also naturally have a view that there's nothing to lose anyway.

If you are seriously considering leaving this life, then there is no harm in skydiving, you might as well, what is there to lose if you're already seriously contemplating leaving?

Psychologically, skydiving is very much a dance with death, which you are already doing anyway internally by playing with the idea of suicide, so you might as well confront it with something like skydiving. Because when you are faced with that very real possibility that the parachute might not come out, when it is unknown whether or not you will live, then you will pretty quickly know what you truly prefer. If you really want that parachute to come out, then you will know deeply within you, that you want to live.

When that parachute does come out, to slow down your fall and give you a pleasant gliding experience back to the earth, you will experience gratitude for being alive and any drama about suicide will naturally stop, because every cell of your body lives through that intense experience and never forgets it.

After I hit rock bottom and overcame the phase of everything being hell, to jump out of an aeroplane with skydiving and accepted the fact that I wanted to live, then even the smallest things made me feel happy, small things and simple things in life that others took for granted.

A beautiful insect landing on a blade of grass. A swan gracefully dipping it's bill into the water as it floated upon a calm still lake that was like glass; reflecting the clear blue sky. A flower blossoming in the sun as a bee gently lands upon it's petal. I appreciated life much more because just about anything was good compared to what I had been through.

From then on, I still had many hardships and challenges because I hadn't gained full understanding of the root of my own mind at that point, as I do now.

But at least I knew I wouldn't ever cross that line to the irreversible action of suicide which would have impacted far more than just my own life.

As I started to realise who I am, my immense value and the profound significance of what I had to contribute to humanity.

I saw that if I did leave, then It would not only have impacted my immediate family, but also the whole human family in a big way.

Because everyone would have missed out on all that I have to offer.

There would never have been the natural cure for mental illness, it would have changed the entire course of the human species to a path of ignorance and unawareness and all of humanity would have lost out big time on my gifts of which I can't entirely disclose to you just yet.

I have heard many people often say to each other and to me throughout my life, *"never give up on your self"*. However, I don't agree with them, because I did have a point in time where I did give up, and that's what made all the difference.

To be clear, it wasn't my life that I was giving up on, I came to see and understand that it was the detrimental *"story of me"* and all of it's detrimental thoughts of doubts, worries, fears, negativity and limitations that I needed to give up on. It was the very identity construct itself, carrying the baggage and all of the drama of depression and suicidal thoughts emotions and behaviours that I needed to give up on.

From then on, I simply chose, that the one with the thoughts and feelings of suicide was no longer mine to carry. I chose to let go of that character, it died with the past and I was able to carry on with my life without the thoughts and feelings of suicide ruining my day.

This is important, especially when it comes to something like suicide, because giving up on the *"suicidal self"* is absolutely necessary in order to overcome it.

Through my journey of suffering, I came to understand that the only real way out from that suffering was by going IN to the source of it. I came to realise through self inquiry meditation that it's not about giving up, but about giving IN.

To direct our attention inwards to resolve and dissolve the drama by looking inwards at the source of the drama which always belongs to an identity construct. I highly recommend giving up on that detrimental suicidal identity. Because when we give up on that internal identity carrying all of the drama and problems in the first place, then what remains is who we really are without those problems and drama.
When you give up on your *"Self"* that's when you can discover the real you.
Gradually, with self inquiry meditation I could clearly see that the *"suicidal one"* isn't who I really am at all, and nor did it have to be anyone else, if only they knew what I knew.

I came to understand that tough times can be a blessing in disguise, it is all a matter of how we view them and deal with them by shifting our perception to see what can be learnt and gained from each and every challenge that we face.

This is especially true when we create our present to be wonderful, this is what I experienced when I later went on to do the necessary inner work to know the way to experience enlightenment.

I then saw that every rung on that ladder that contributed to bring me to that awareness and state of being was a teacher, each played it's part and that I could only be grateful for each and every one, no matter how many blisters or splinters that each rung gave me.

Now, when I look back on that suicidal sense of self and all of the sufferings that I experienced, I can feel grateful for them all, because they were stepping stones that I was meant to go through and experience at that time as part of the journey.

If I hadn't, then I'd never be in a position to be able to help others and understand this process to the degree that I do now.
You wouldn't be reading what you are reading now, everything that I went through made me very strong and I'm grateful for that. There is a purpose, value and light in the darkness of all challenges.

I understand now that lived experience is so invaluable, that it is the highest education, that no book or academic course of the mainstream system could ever compare with it, nor teach anything any where near to the degree of knowledge and understanding that I had gained from living through all that I have lived through and experienced.

People with lived experience have much more knowledge and value to give to anyone going through mental illness, and are much more effective in helping people overcome their psychological and emotional challenges.

Anyone I've ever heard of recovering to a reasonable degree from mental illness always found their best support and solutions outside of the mainstream mental health systems, whether that's by yoga, meditation, healthy food and diet, improving fitness with regular exercise, team sports, time in nature and more.
This is especially true from my view because I know what it takes to truly cure even diagnosed mental illness all the way, which even to

this day psyches are telling people that those diagnosed illnesses are incurable, however, I am a living proof that they are very wrong.

Quite frankly all of the solutions and answers to well-being and great mental health are always found outside of the mainstream mental health systems.

CHAPTER 2:

WHAT'S WRONG WITH THE CURRENT SYSTEM?

For many decades, and at the time of this book's release, there is an immense amount of change that still needs to occur within the mental health system.

I will be discussing this in much more depth and detail in up and coming parts of this series. For now, we will be focusing mostly on what specifically needs changing in regards to suicide prevention.

I am very much someone who would rather focus on the solutions to things, however, in order to solve and improve things with the mental health system, it is important that we first identify and understand what needs solving and improving.

Although many mental health professionals may have a good heart and mean well, people who went into the field genuinely wanting to make a positive change to peoples lives and society as a whole. It doesn't change the nature and structures of the dysfunctional systems that they are trained to work in.

Because the fact of the matter is that many education system programs that create psychiatrists, have in fact been heavily funded by big pharmaceutical companies pouring millions of dollars into them.

One simply needs to understand that those people and companies are seeking a return on their investment. That the money they put into those education systems, will result in bigger returns on the other side of the persons certificate. Not only in the form of money, but also in the form of power and control. This causes education systems to be compromised and specially tailored to fulfill the interests and agendas of those people and companies that have invested their money into them.

It is because of this, that Psychiatrists themselves have become like a product of big pharma. Ultimately it is about control, money and what those behind big pharma perceive and think to be a position of power. It is designed to further their own selfish agendas which has been at the expense and detriment of all human life and well-being, including their own if they were aware enough to realise it.

Mental health professionals have been groomed and trained by these compromised education systems. Psychiatrists are mostly only taught what those investors want to teach them in order to further their business.

This severely limits what is allowed within their scope of practice, which in turn also severely limits the degree to which they are capable of truly helping people.

Their education trains and conditions them to be a particular way, so that the prime directive of therapy and treatment results in labeling people with made up diagnosis and putting them on medication.
This in return achieves their objective for control, while also increasing the sales and dependence on their medications, ultimately keeping people stuck, wasting their time and lives trapped in the mental health system as lifelong customers.

Therefore, rather than achieving and fulfilling any true and lasting well-being for the vulnerable person and humanity as a whole, they do the opposite, making more people unwell and only results in the fulfillment of those pharmaceutical companies and their destructive and controlling agendas.

This has impacted the kinds of practices, procedures, treatments and outcomes that the mental health professionals have been able to undertake with clients, this has also impacted the way by which the overall mental health system operates.

For example, when the primary objective of the psychiatrist becomes one of reaching an outcome of so called "treatment" for the client; in the form of medications. This has often meant drugging the person up, so that they are numb and docile enough to then be swept under the rug for a while. Just long enough so that they aren't a problem, and so that the psych can put a tick in the box to make it look like they are doing something productive and meaningful about it.

However, these medications are not designed to be solutions, in many cases they come with side effects and symptoms which then cause more health problems and conditions. In such a case, just like a salesman the psychiatrist is trained to go for the "up sell" whereby the new health problems such as anxiety and depression give the psychiatrist a reason to tell the person that they require additional medications for those new side effects and symptoms.

It is by design that this approach often leads to a growing list of detrimental medications for the person to become a dependent and life long customer of big pharma.

It is in their vested interests to keep people unwell, because keeping people unwell maintains their business.

This is also one of the reasons why they create diagnosis labels to stick on people and maintain the illness through the person's identification with those labels. The act of giving people a diagnosis has multiple benefits for those who are corrupt, for example, it is designed to diminish the credibility of people who witness and experience otherworldly experiences such as UFO sightings, psychic experiences and Extra-terrestrial phenomena or other mystical and spiritual experiences that may challenge the status quo, wake people up and release them from the grips of control.
The convenience of a labeled diagnosis is designed to not only discredit anything that they and their third parties wish to remain secret and hidden, but it also gives them more of a reason to push medications onto people.

Fear has often been used as a tool and mechanism for manipulation, control and leverage by businesses, institutions, mainstream media and governments, often all working together to try and achieve a particular outcome, which has often only been for their own selfish interests and agendas. This has nearly always been to the detriment and at the expense of the whole, making stupid decisions that go against the will of the people, disregarding human rights and well-being, ultimately holding all of humanity back from realising it's highest potential.

For example, on the smaller and much less harmful scale, fear may be used by a business selling bloated anti-virus software, having their potential customers believe that they are unsafe without their product using fear as a tool to increase sales.

On a much larger global scale and much more detrimental scale, we have seen fear used relentlessly by the media, working for the vested interests of big pharmaceutical companies to sell their highly questionable vaccines to Governments and the people.

Vaccines that are untested, with undisclosed ingredients that are unsafe, harmful and highly detrimental. All while trying to make people believe that they are going to be sick or even die if they don't have them, which of course is a lie.

This would then lead to the implementation of new nonsensical restrictive and controlling rules and regulations being imposed upon the people, trying to push their controlling agendas, telling them that it's for their own good and so called "safety" while doing the opposite trying to take away fundamental rights and freedoms with a complete disregard for the health and well-being of the people.

Religion is another example that for millennia has often been used for manipulation, control and leverage, for example selling people a fear of not being accepted and included, out-casting them with a label and trying to sell them a fear of going to hell or some other damnation if they don't submit to following and believing in the same religious ideology.

Just like these examples, the use of fear as a tool and mechanism for manipulation, control and leverage within the mental health system is no different.

One of the key things to true recovery from suicidal thoughts feelings and mental illness in general, requires us to block out the so called "professionals" detrimental opinions and ignore their attempts to sell us fears that if we don't take their meds then something terrible is going to happen. The psychiatrists have also often used fear tactics in order to keep the person under control and dependent on them. They would say things like *"In my professional opinion, I strongly advise that you keep taking this medication, if you don't, then I'm afraid that there's a high risk that your condition will worsen."*

This is one example of negligence and misuse of their influential positions of perceived authority by using these manipulative fear tactics on vulnerable people in this way.

They are trained to do this and say these things, and they are also in a sense held at ransom by the education systems that also use fear tactics on them too, which keeps them in line to make sure that they follow the formula. Because if they don't, then their rights to continue so called "professional practice" are threatened.

All of this results in not providing what's truly in the best interests of the client and what is truly needed for their health and well-being.

This has then often been followed up by the person being subject to what I call the "revolving door system" which we most often see especially in public mental health systems. This is where psychiatrists would leave and be replaced by some other random psychiatrist, often only fresh out of university with little to no life experience. This is where you find yourself having to explain everything about you and your story over and over again to each new person, only for them to be substituted by someone new, psyche after psyche like a merry-go-round with each one trying to sell you a new medication.

This dysfunctional process alone has been the cause for many psychological and emotional problems, the system itself is what mostly causes problems for people.

It has been a system which has had no sincere care about the client and their well-being, in many cases the client has only been treated like a number, handed onto the next psych to try some new drugs like a guinea pig, only to become someone else's problem. This constant disruption of shuffling psyches and medications has caused much disruption and stress to anyone trying to make some meaningful progress for their well-being.

The mental health professional's trained obedience and conditioning has caused them to automatically risk the safety, privacy and well-being of clients. This has most directly and adversely impacted the people they claim to "treat" and their families.

For example, when it comes to those who are suicidal, we can see that the health professional is trained to make poor and irrational decisions.

People who express that they experience suicidal thoughts and emotions, have naturally been subject to the poor practices of the corrupt and incompetent mental health systems, which have been incredibly insensitive and cruel. In fact, it's disgusting how people have been treated, because often when people are expressing those things, they are reaching out to someone while they are in a vulnerable state, in the hope that they will receive some sense of understanding, empathy, compassion, and care from that person.
However, the approach of the failed system has been to freak out, call the police and lock them up in a cell at the mere mention of someone having suicidal thoughts and feelings. This has then been followed up by the so called "treatment" of putting them under involuntary

drug treatment against their will, which involves forcing detrimental mind numbing medications down their throats or injecting them with a needle to make them numb like zombies.

This is all because they attempted to reach out for help, wanting to communicate with someone to express how they have been feeling. Only to be met with ignorance and misunderstanding.

There is something horribly wrong with any system that practices such a disgusting, heartless and in-humane procedure on such vulnerable people. In my eyes it is actually criminal, because it is a form of abuse and it only makes things worse for those people by locking them up and forcing them on questionable medications against their will. It shows a complete lack of understanding, and a complete lack of emotional intelligence in the form of compassion and empathy.

After such a traumatic and in-humane experience of treatment, do you really think that these people would ever want to tell anyone in the system again that they are feeling suicidal? Of course not, because they know the consequences of doing so, which is abuse and mistreatment, so they feel that they have no choice but to stay silent and bottle it up inside, allowing it to gradually eat away at them, feeling alone with no help in sight and nobody to turn to.

This detrimental approach adopted by the mental health system only results in people not being able to trust anyone or talk to anyone about their true thoughts, feelings and experiences.
They become too fearful of being judged, called crazy, and mistreated with forced mind numbing medications, dobbed in to others just for the mere mention of experiencing suicidal thoughts. The suicidal person then feels like they can't talk to anyone about their challenges and issues, which is exactly what they need to be able to do.

This is one of the reasons why more than 50% of suicides have been from people who had previously received mental health support from professionals.

Problems inevitably resurface again at a later date for the person experiencing suicidal thoughts emotions and behaviours, because just like a weed that re-surfaces in the garden when it is not dealt with properly at the root, the suicidal person's issues also resurface because they haven't truly been dealt with and resolved at the core root; which is internal.

It doesn't take a genius to know, that if the source of the depression and suicidal feelings has come from within them, then the solution is also found within them. Not with mind numbing medications and not with a corrupt and broken mental health system whose only purpose has been to act as a sales shop-front for the horribly corrupt pharmaceutical companies which quite frankly should be held accountable for their crimes against humanity.

Quite simply put, the mental health system is clearly an incompetent and failed system. It needs a complete transformation on every level. Its a system which has been designed to make mental health professionals immediately react out of misunderstanding, assumptions, with ignorance and fear.

Their decisions are irrational and driven by fear in order to adhere to various protocols and codes of conduct such as *"risk of harm"*, *"duty of care"* and *"mandatory reporting"*.

However this fear is always founded in "what could happen", it is non-existential. As the great master yogi and mystic Sadhguru has also pointed out, quote:

"The Fear is simply because you're not living with life, you're living in your mind, your fear is always about what's

going to happen next, that means your fear is always about that which does not exist, if your fear is about the non-existent, your fear is 100% imaginary, if you're suffering the non-existential, we call that insanity, so people may be in just socially accepted levels of insanity, but if you're afraid or you're suffering anything that does not exist, it amounts to insanity."

With this awareness, it's very easy to see the profound irony of the situation; that it is actually most of the mental health professionals and those who train them that are the ones who are mentally ill.

Additionally, most mental health professionals don't have any lived experience themselves of what the suicidal person is truly going through, so they mostly don't know how to properly deal with those suicidal people and their situations anyway.

In reference to the following image called:
"Image 1: The Warrior",
I will use the following analogy to further illustrate my point.

Many of the so called "Professionals", (psychiatrists in particular) who are without lived experience. Who in times of need try to tell those of us about how to cope with suicidal thoughts and emotions then offer medication, are like a weak and cowardly salesman who beckons to the traveling Warrior on the pathway up the mountain.

That, despite their lack of experience in slaying Monsters, they stop the warrior to tell them all about how to slay a Monster that they've never even seen, dwelling deep inside a cave that they've never even stepped in, using only their highly recommended and "psych approved" pocket knife in the form of medications as the so called "treatment" that they've never even used or tested themselves.

IMAGE 1: THE WARRIOR

Above: Image 1 – The Warrior

The suicidal person needs someone to talk to, without them being judged and mistreated with detrimental medications by incompetent and tyrannical mental health systems.
They need to be supported in an environment that provides true privacy, dignity, respect, and safety, that is truly caring, nurturing, full of empathy, compassion and understanding.

This means with someone who knows what they are actually talking about with sufficient lived experience because they have already slayed that Monster themselves. This is also someone who can listen to them without judgement and help them truly work through and resolve the challenging issues that they face.

This is easier for someone with lived experience, because the person with lived experience needed to be listened to on their journey too. They know what it's like to not be heard and to not be respected, therefore they naturally understand the importance and value of listening to the person properly in a way that no mainstream education course can teach.

If we were to apply the mental health system's practices and procedures to the scenario that I have just described to you, then the situation has been the equivalent of the traveling warrior having a law laid down on them, where they have been forced to buy the pathetic little pocket knife (i.e medications) from the shady dealer (the Psychiatrist) before they can go and face the Monster.(i.e internal challenges)

This is just one of the many way's by which psychiatrists in particular have now lost just about all credibility, because more and more people are now starting to wake up and realise that they are merely just drug pushers for big pharma at the expense of human rights and well-being.

This is only touching the surface of what I will be exposing throughout this series.

CHAPTER 3:

UNDERSTANDING SUICIDE, THE CAUSES OF SUICIDE

Suicidal thoughts and emotions can begin for some people as a bit of a dramatic act, where they might be feeling unhappy and depressed, but not really to the degree and point of sincerely wanting to leave their life.

In many cases some people like to be dramatic and put on a performance for attention and to see how much others will care about them when they express those things. They are testing the waters, because they feel depressed, insufficient, unheard and unloved. When they don't receive the response from others that they are looking for to indicate some level of love and care, then this may re-enforce their detrimental and depressing thoughts and beliefs of insufficiency and lack of value about themselves leading to greater degrees of depression.

This perception of non-caring and non-loving behaviour from others causes them to think that it justifies them doing some form of self harm, creating the suicidal drama to become something more and more real for them. However, once they start playing with that idea of being suicidal and identify their personality with it as "someone who is suicidal", it then becomes something much more serious and very real for them.

In all cases that I can think of, the thoughts, emotions and action of suicide comes from someone who is unable to see beyond their current situation, like being stuck in a dense and misty fog, unable to see a way forward to the next step. They think that in order to escape from their suffering, the answer to all of their problems is to take their own life, that from their point of view, in that moment of clouded vision, death seems to be a better option than living.

Suicide in many cases comes about by a psychological equation, where the person's happiness and reasons for living the life, are outweighed by the person's degree of suffering and the reasons for leaving the life.

Depression

Depression is considered to be one of the most common kinds of mental illness and it is also linked with many suicides in some way or another. It is very rare to find someone who is feeling suicidal, without them also feeling some degree of depression.

Depression may come about for many reasons, it can be about both outside situations and inside situations which are one in the same, because in most cases outside situations are a result of the internal situation and how well we deal with outside situations also depends on how stable our inside situation is.

Some examples of how depression can come about for people are as follows.

Depression can be the result of numerous detrimental habits such as alcohol consumption or eating unhealthy food, for example it is now well known that having a high sugar consumption alone can increase the likelihood of depression. Video game addictions that result in late nights create a disruption to natural sleep patterns that bring the person out of alignment with natures cycles and rhythms, leading to a lack of natural vitamin D from the Sun, insufficient exercise and a lack of meaningful social interaction and connection beyond the screen.

A person's environment can also impact their well-being, so long term exposure to toxic behaviours and self destructive people such as alcoholics can have a detrimental impact to the well-being.

A person may be depressed from psychological means such as by the definition and narrative of the media and other irresponsible people who have sold them a lie about *"how the world is"*, who fed them a whole range of things to be depressed about, worried about and afraid of, things which may not even be true.

Depression may come about by the reckless detrimental actions and decisions of ignorant and arrogant people in positions of perceived authority. Such as controlling and power hungry Governments who impose their silly agendas with oppressive and unfair rules and restrictions upon the people at the expense of human rights and well-being.

Depression could occur because of someone comparing themselves with others, being rejected by others, not fitting in or feeling a sense of belonging. Depression, comes to those that identify themselves as someone who's not good enough, buying into detrimental thoughts about themselves, beating themselves up over the relentless noise of their own mind. Where the person has been raised in unawareness of how the mind works, not knowing how to deal with their mental noise and mind chatter. The poor conditioning left unchecked as their well-being gradually deteriorated over time.

Depression is the result of being too identified with the artificial personality construct sense of "self", where parts of the person's "story of me" doesn't sit well with them or where the person has bought into something about themselves that is detrimental and may not even be true.
The person is unable to love and fully accept who they are most often because they don't yet realise or know who they truly are, only who they have been taught to believe they are and define themselves to be. Resulting in the person living as an unhealthy, diminished, disempowered and devalued individual.

The depressed person is not able to recognise their own individual value and potential. The significance and value of their uniqueness, their life, who they can become and what their life and world can be. They look at things through a limited pessimistically distorted and foggy lens point of view, shrouding their own vision to only see negativity and limitation. Looking out with a negatively oriented view of themselves, their world and their life situation.

Depression may come about due to the person not living with the present, crying over spilt milk i.e events of the past that one holds regrets over such as lost opportunities and poor choices, things that can't be changed or undone.

Depression can be managed and resolved by our daily actions, i.e having enough rest, receiving enough sunlight for vitamin D, living by a healthy diet, doing consistent exercise week after week, creating more face to face social opportunities and engagement, having more time with nature and developing other healthy habits can all contribute to overcoming depression.

If we do the right things then depression is easy to overcome, you can't drink alcohol every week, eat junk food, never do any exercise and stay up late most nights then expect to be 100% happy and jumping out of your skin to live a full and rich life. It requires a conscious decision and choice to be well.

By addressing the depression and the numerous things that may cause and contribute to depression, then we can greatly reduce the number of people who are thinking, feeling and behaving in a suicidal manner.

Although there is the obvious cause for suicide being heavily linked to depression (which we will cover shortly), not all suicide is the result of depression.
Some forms of suicide are 100% the result of intentional brainwashing, some examples include the Jones town massacre of November 18th 1978 in the United States of America and various incidents of suicide bombings have been a result of ideological and religious indoctrination, where belief systems are carried by the person to cause them to take actions that they otherwise wouldn't take if they didn't adopt those brainwashed belief systems.

Nobody is ever born suicidal, It's not human nature at all to be suicidal, suicide is unnatural. No other creature on the planet that I know of commits suicide on purpose by choice. It's not something that is built into the natural genetics. It's not part of our natural course of growth like growing nails, hair or teeth, nor is it like a limb or body part that grows naturally.

It is from this awareness, that we can easily recognise that suicide is external to us as humans, that it is something which is introduced into the mind from elsewhere, that it's something which first needs to be picked up as an idea on the mental level from the outside world for it to become a thing.
The idea of Suicide is something which is formulated and programmed into the person with conditioning over time.

In most cases, the idea of suicide is introduced by someone else speaking about it, where the person picks up the idea from the detrimental influence of television shows, where a story line speaks about it and suggests it in some way or another, or the evening news irresponsibly decides to broadcast a tragic event that nobody can do anything about. Which they have always done intentionally to distract, depress and dis-empower their viewers, after such a tragic and sad story they would then give the viewers an advertisement encouraging the viewer to buy something that can give them a temporary dopamine hit such as ads for chocolate or fast food to compensate for their new depressed, hopeless and unhappy mood.

This is just one example of the countless brainwashing tactics of the media that have had a detrimental impact on the mental health and well-being of humanity. This is because many have been unaware of the importance of what they allow into their mind.
Thoughts are like food, they can be harmonious, healthy and constructive and they can be detrimental and deadly, it all depends on how we approach them and how much of our attention and energy we give to them.

Responsibility is a great and valuable thing, because with responsibility it means that we have the choice and power in how we choose to respond.

People have choices about what they allow into their minds. When it comes to television or harmful social media, the power of the viewer is with their choice to not watch those things, while the media is also responsible for what they put on the airwaves, everyone is responsible for their choices.

My point with this being that like many things, it is only by the persons investment of thoughts, emotions and energies into the idea of suicide which allow it to ever become a thing. We can simply choose not to do that, this is important to understand because for anything to become an action, it is first a thought, an idea and only if that thought is nourished and given our energy and attention; can it ever become a thing.

CHAPTER 4:

FOR THOSE WHO HAVE LOST

Grieving the loss of loved ones is never easy, grief is a matter of the heart and the heart needs time to heal.

If you are someone who has had your life shattered by the loss of a loved one, I will have you know that you're not alone, there are many others out there who share your experience. Be gentle with yourself and give yourself the time and space that you need to heal. Time in nature can be very beneficial for this.

You can and will get through this, and your ability to do so will depend upon what you decide to do with this experience. We all need each others experience to collectively grow and make this a better world. Don't let the experience of losing your loved one be wasted. There is value in this experience and challenge that you have been given and it can be turned into something beneficial for all if you are willing to let it. Let go of any guilt or shame that you may be carrying about it.

One of the great gifts to come out of all of this, may be that from your own journey of healing and recovery, you will be able to begin the mission to help many others who go through a similar experience.

The following are some unique and beneficial suggestions that I know can be very helpful in the healing process.

Apache Tears

Above: "Apache Tears"
The Apache women grieved the loss of their husbands and sons in battle, they shed so many tears until their tears turned to stone. This gemstone is named after the legend, it was used by the Apache who knew that it's properties contained natures gift and intelligence for helping them to cope with grief and sorrow.

Psychic Mediums
I ask you to put aside any doubtful, skeptical and conditioned judgements that you may have about the idea of psychic mediums and only make a valued judgement based on your direct lived experience.

Psychic mediums who specialize in contact with those who have passed can be very beneficial in bringing closure and exchange of knowledge and information that can greatly aid in the healing process going forward.

It is important to discern and know who is legitimate, and who genuinely has been granted these great gifts.

I have witnessed the skill and ability of true psychic mediums who are spiritually gifted to perceive and channel profound things from the other side, exchanging messages from those who have passed that can easily be confirmed for their legitimacy and accuracy.

Alicia Bickett is one such example of a medium in Australia who I would highly recommend seeing for anyone going through the grieving process of loss of loved ones who wishes for communication with those who have passed in order to bring healthy closure. There are many other top quality mediums from many other countries around the world, it is up to you to do your research and find the right person who feels right for you.

I do know grief, however, this book is not about grief, it is about the Solution to Suicide. Such grief of losing a loved one specifically to suicide, is not in my own personal lived experience, so I will not comment any further on this specific subject at this time.

However, I will encourage those who do have it in their lived experience and who overcame it, to find each other, to talk and/or write about it and share it. This will help others by giving a clearer insight into the process of how to overcome it too.

CHAPTER 5:

FOR THOSE WHO ARE THINKING AND FEELING SUICIDAL

Many people who have gone through and are going through suicidal thoughts and feelings have immense value that they are often not even aware of. For those of you reading this now, who have been struggling and battling with the thoughts and feelings of suicide, then this message is especially for you.

I acknowledge that some of you reading this are going through the rough seas, that some of you may be hanging on by the very last thread, and that the thoughts of suicide on the surface may seem like a very reasonable option considering the current circumstances and situation that you find yourself in. However, before you choose to take any irreversible action of leaving this life, as someone who has overcome all of this, I ask you to consider the following.

You may feel like you are a miner, who has been digging for a long time down a deep, dark and lonely tunnel, where no-one can see you or hear you, down towards the centre of your soul, hitting rock bottom, where you have raised the water levels from your tears, now up to your chest, swamped in your sadness, where now instead of the sound of the drops in your dark cave you only hear the sound of silence because your tears have run dry, as you have shed every last tear that you could.

Your head torch has run out of batteries and you can't see a way out of your struggles and misery, thinking that all is lost, looking like there is no way forward. You replay over in your mind all the reasons why you feel the way that you do, events, people, circumstances, regrets, fears, losses and grief. You may have many valid reasons for feeling the way that you do.

You think that you only have two options, the first being to break the body and leave or the second being to live on in a world of misery, pain and despair, unable to accept how things are or forgive yourself. Thinking that life happens to you as a victim, thinking that the struggle and suffering is all there is. But there is a third option, and that is to stay strong, to not give up, to overcome, and to rise above. To make your dreams a reality, to become the greatest version of you, to live the best life that you can live, to be and make the differences and changes in the world that truly improve things for everyone.
There is no doubt that you have something special to offer to this world otherwise you wouldn't be here. You too have something stirring within you that is for the purpose of making this world a better place than when you arrived.

I know that the challenge you may be currently facing may seem like a giant mountain too big and heavy to overcome, but this mountain that you face is only ever as big as what you make it out to be in your own mind. It doesn't have to be as big as what your mind has made it out to be, and you will be surprised at how strong and capable you really are once you make the decision and choice and choose to make positive changes to live a great life. It is a choice that you can make right now from this presence.

If you were not capable of overcoming and rising above the challenge that you are given, then it would not have been given to you.

There is a purpose and reason that you face this challenge of overcoming suicidal thoughts and feelings, it is an opportunity that you give to yourself for your advancement.

Your story of suffering and struggle was like a stepping stone, a rung on the ladder. It was a part of the journey to get you to where you need to go, and just like when we are stepping on the stones crossing a creek, not all stones in life are stable, and not all rungs on the ladder in life are without their splinters, but you can and you will get past this and overcome this to live a great life if you choose to allow yourself to do so.

Your darkness and difficult experiences and situation is not to be viewed as negative. Understand that your challenges and darkness are all part of the process towards your transformation.

This process of transformation that you are going through, is similar in nature to the transformation of a caterpillar who is becoming a butterfly.

No caterpillar ever became a butterfly without the darkness of the cocoon first. So be grateful for your darkness and embrace your darkness, because darkness is the womb from which all brilliance is born.

Embraced in this darkness, in the cocoon of transformation, comes the time when one is ready to emerge, breaking limitations and giving birth to the new and brilliant version, ready to claim your divine birthright for greatness, becoming who you really are.

There is a purpose to all of it. In all transformation there is a process that is like death and rebirth. We can see symbols of this in nature everywhere, for example, after there are bush fires, new growth sprouts forth that is lush and green. Some plants even depend upon the natural fire and are designed for being subject to the fire in order to reproduce such as the fern tree in Australia.

When you get through all of this, you will be more brilliant and even stronger than ever before, so that you too can shine as a guiding light for others, raising others up and out from their darkness until they too shine bright.

For the brightest of Stars, the Darkness is home.

We cannot force a Butterfly from it's Cocoon before it's time to be a butterfly, so be gentle with yourself, enjoy the process and journey. This transformation will take as long as it needs to, to be ok with the cocoon, be ok with the darkness and soon, the splendid glory of the sun will rise within you and shine it's beautiful rays of light through you and out into the world.

After going through this process, you will feel great peace, unburdened by anything of the past, dignified, beautiful and free, as you begin this new chapter of your life. At some point in all of our human experiences, we are all called to face the darkness one way or another.

The darkness is not something to fear, it is not dirty, bad, negative or any other conditioned label that your society or religion may have you believe. The Darkness is your friend. Within that deep darkness resides the space and place for true inner growth and powerful transformation. The darkness is the space for the destruction and cleansing of what no longer serves us and it is also the space for the creation of bright and powerful stars.

I'm sure that many people by now have heard the common analogy that it is the pressure upon a piece of coal which can turn it into a strong, valuable and unbreakable diamond.
I've thought more deeply about this, to go further and deeper in understanding the significance of our relationship to this process.

There is a peculiar relationship between the human body and diamonds, because, the human body itself is a carbon based life form and diamonds are also from carbon too. Therefore this analogy is rather significant to understand because we literally share this potential of alchemical transformation.

When a star reaches the end of it's life, it goes through a natural process of destruction to become a super nova explosion. It is the pressure of that immense and magnificently powerful super nova explosion, which creates the indestructible natural black diamonds known as "carbonados".
It is an immense destruction far greater than anything we have ever experienced on earth, but still, the black diamond survives that extreme pressure to remain as a hard diamond, a survivor.
Through our own darkness we face great pressures. Any hardships and challenges we face as humans in life are also a way of strengthening us, as we too have the opportunity to become stronger like diamonds.

It is by our conscious decision and choice, that we can choose at any moment to be like a piece of coal or a diamond.

Humpty Dumpty Vs Gumby

"Humpty dumpty sat on a wall, humpty dumpty had a great fall, all the Kings horses and all the Kings men, couldn't put humpty together again."

I'm sure that many of you have heard this well known nursery rhyme before. Humpty Dumpty is an egg and as the nursery rhyme describes, when an egg falls off the wall and shatters on the ground, the shell is broken and it's not coming back together so easily. On the other hand, another well known character from an old TV series called "Gumby" is much more flexible and malleable. When he is pulled apart he can reform himself back together again.

It's his nature to do so, my point being, that we can choose to either be like Humpty dumpty and be fragile and crack easily and let things hurt us and shatter us or we can choose to be like Gumby and transform ourselves and our challenging situation when things aren't well, to be flexible, malleable and transformative.
This is also the nature of the universe, to be regenerative, malleable., transformable, because everything is energy and this is the nature of energy. When we are learning to walk for the first time, inevitably we all fall at one point or another, but we don't just stay on the ground.
If we stay down, we are defeated, not by life, but by our choice to stay down.

It is our nature to rise up, to get ourselves up off the floor, and keep going. We persevere through our challenges and adversities until we overcome them and we have the opportunity through these challenges to become stronger and wiser if we choose to learn from them.

The choice is always in our hands to live a great life. We all have this choice right now in this presence.

CHAPTER 6:
RECOGNIZING YOUR TRUE VALUE

The fundamental foundation for wellness is in our everyday awareness and actions, as previously mentioned, depression is well known as a common link with most suicides.

However, suicide can be much more complex than just depression. While there are those things that can greatly improve one's well-being, for some people the pain and suffering is too much to even have any incentive of wanting to alleviate depression or begin changing their habits and making healthy choices.

In order to achieve those things, one needs a reason to and this requires a shift in perception to see the reasons for living. To be empowered by recognizing the true value and significance of their own existence. To recognise the value of the unique being that they are which can never be compared with nor ever replaced.

Recognizing your true value.

Depression is also a result of not understanding nor recognizing your true value, because society has conditioned people to look to the ego identity and the material in order to measure and compare that perceived sense of "value".

True value is found in our unique expression of creation on a much deeper level for who and what we were created to be. All of us in this way are infinitely unique and incomparable. If there was any true measurement of value then from my perspective and experience it is regarding the soul evolution and advancement from one life to the next, though I will discuss that in later parts of the series.

We all have a purpose and reason for being here on this world and it's very unlikely that you came to this world just so that you would experience suicide.

You are a valued part of the whole and you have a place in the universe that is meant for you.
Even though your mission and purpose may not be so clear to you just yet, understand that you are here for a reason and that you are needed. There is a reason and purpose that you are here and have this life, even if that reason and purpose were to be as simple as living your life in peacefulness to maintain that vibration of inspiration for others on the earth.

The idea of unworthiness is also only a thought, a belief system that some choose to buy into. It has no power over you unless you choose to believe that it does.
If you were not worthy of your life and existence then it would not have been gifted to you. You are a part of creation, made out of divine material, literally made of the same material as stars. You are a valued member of the human family, of existence, and just like a star, it is

your purpose to shine as brightly as you can into the world, not with your ego but with your genuine spirit of who you really are.

This unique form that you are, that nobody else can be, has never been here before, and it will never come again.
You are a unique being of creation which can never be replaced. That alone is worth living for. That alone is valuable, that even what may appear to be imperfections, that the unconscious society thinks and was taught to believe are imperfections, are in fact perfections of uniqueness.
We all represent something infinitely unique, and that is naturally intended. To judge the appearance of others is to judge an expression of "God". Accept and love the unique being that you are because you are the only one who can fill those shoes and be this unique being that you are.
It is simply the truth, that you are rarer than the rarest of gems, one of a kind, a priceless jewel. You are irreplaceable.

This isn't just a bunch of nice warm and fuzzy sounding words just to try and make you feel better. It is the truth and you will naturally feel better because deep down you know that I am speaking the truth and nobody can take this truth away from you.
You are a one of a kind, worthy of your existence and valuable; Own this truth.

CHAPTER 7:
THE SOLUTION TO SUICIDE

It is a gift in disguise that this experience of mental illness and or suicidal thoughts and feelings comes to people, because it demands that one re-directs their attention inwards towards the source of it. This is a great gift, because when one starts to move in that direction to discover the source of their sufferings, then not only will they discover how to overcome all of their challenges and sufferings of all kinds for life, but they will also move towards unlocking the path towards their natural highest potential and greatest life.

Knowing the root and source of the mind, is to know the root and source of all human experience in both ourselves and others.

The key to properly overcoming Suicidal thoughts, emotions and behaviours is this: Overcoming Suicide requires the awareness as to what is really going on within us. It is about confronting the sense of "self" character within, and asking "who is the one who is suicidal?". This is the one who has been creating and entertaining the thoughts, feelings, behaviours and dramas of suicide in the first place. It is about having the awareness to transform it, by internally confronting it. This can be done in the following two ways. Both are important and can be combined together:

1. The first is with **Lived Experiences** such as what I have described in the "my story" section, where I had confronted those suicidal thoughts and feelings by taking the action of Skydiving and countering those thoughts and feelings that were within me by proving to myself that I did in fact want to live. This can be immensely beneficial and also a much more powerful and better way than some of the methods that have been used by the mental health system, such as having the suicidal person sign a no-suicide contract, where they agree with their therapist through written contract that they won't suicide.

This would be a much stronger contract and mean a lot more when it is backed by the person's own confronting lived experience of something like skydiving, where there is the unforgettable memory of having to confront oneself, resulting in a knowingness that one will not suicide.

This doesn't mean that everyone feeling suicidal needs to go skydiving in particular, just that when one has the experience of life being uncertain in some way or another that one appreciates it more.

This could be by swimming with sharks, bunji jumping, or any other extreme situation that presents a certain degree of risk. If the suicidal one is not ok with the risk and not prepared to do these things that may bring fear then it's also extremely beneficial, because depending on the person's willingness to do those things you will soon have your answer as to whether or not they really are suicidal and if deeper down they really want to live.

For the person to say no, it will tell you that deep down the suicidal behaviour isn't 100% serious, because if they were truly suicidal there would be nothing to lose. This is not to discredit what the person is going through by any means, but that to some degree it means that the person is putting on a bit of a dramatic act and so they will need to look inwards at that for why it's happening.

The Lived experience aspect of the solution is about causing that mechanism of appreciation for life to bring greater awareness and realisation to how precious and valuable it is and that it's not to be wasted.

This idea of creating the lived experience can be extremely powerful and plant the seed for lifelong prevention of suicide in the individual. However, it doesn't entirely make one aware of the root cause of it and the awareness as to how it came about, nor how to overcome other potential dramas throughout life that may arise psychologically and emotionally further down the path.

In order to have ultimate transformation and reach such mastery, for complete understanding and resolution, what is needed is to combine the Lived experience and also implement Internal Action with self-inquiry, by addressing the root of any detrimental identities that caused one to get to that point of suicidal ideation.

Which brings us to our second and main point of focus: **Internal Action**

2. Taking **Internal Action** by using **Self Inquiry Meditation**, will not only reveal the truth that those detrimental identities and voices from within you are not you, but it will also give you experiential understanding of who you truly are, removing any limitations for you to live the life that you truly prefer.

With the right kind of internal action, you can discover the source of all thoughts, beliefs, points of view and beyond them all to know the deeper truth of all.

We will be focusing heavily on the internal action aspect of self inquiry, so that you can begin to comprehend how and why it is of the most profound significance, not only for overcoming mental illness and suicide, but also to reach the most advanced levels of psychological and spiritual growth.

I will now share with you the solutions that I had discovered more than 10 years ago from lived experience. Solutions which have come from a deeper place of discovery which makes all the difference which will enable all of humanity to truly solve this once and for all.

CHAPTER 8:

THE SEQUENCE TREE – IDENTITY, THOUGHTS, EMOTIONS AND ACTIONS.

"We are what we think. All that we are arises with our thoughts. With our thoughts, we make the world."
- *Gautama Buddha*

All actions that are taken in the world, depend upon the level and quality of the thoughts and emotions fueling and driving them into existence.

Suicide is an action and the source of all action is thought and emotion.

Thoughts and emotions are the cause and fuel for all human actions in the world.

Therefore, we come to see and realise that all actions of suicide are preventable and can be overcome simply because all internal thoughts and emotions can be overcome.

To overcome, de-program and ultimately cure mental illness and suicide, we need to first understand the importance of the building blocks, mechanisms and processes behind them, to understand that our thoughts and our emotions are what becomes our behaviours and actions.

I will illustrate this now for you visually with the following concept in Image 2: The Sequence Tree.

IMAGE 2: THE SEQUENCE TREE

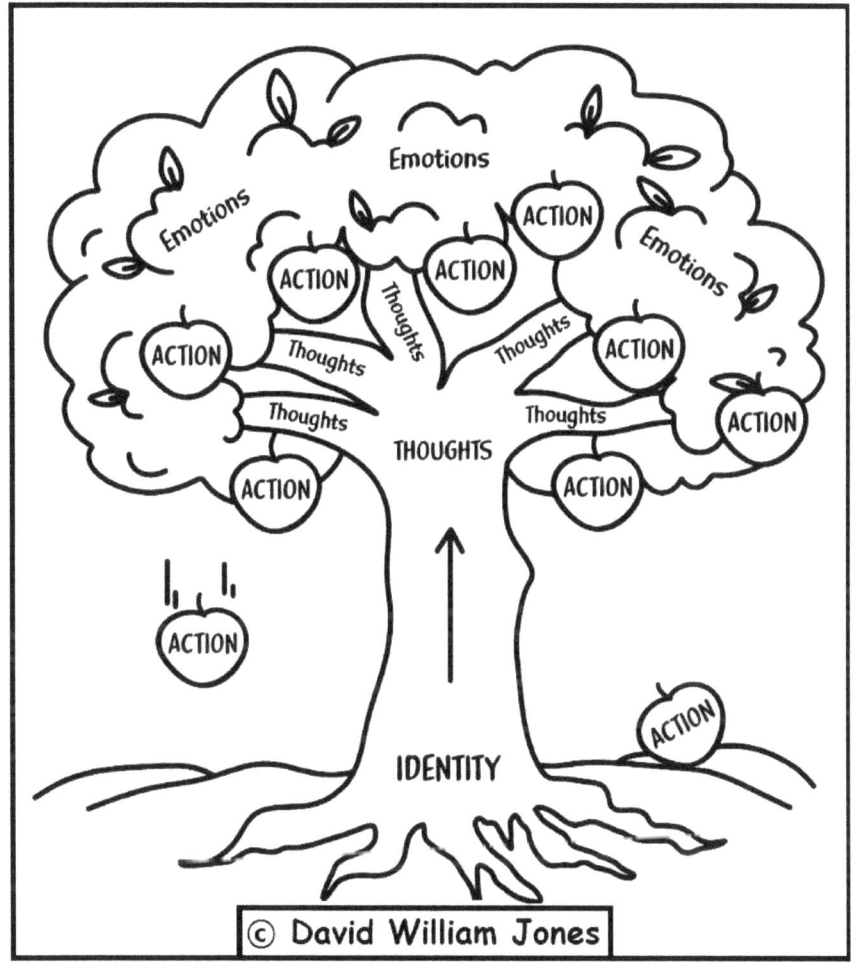

Above: Image 2 – The Sequence Tree

In this image we can see each part of the tree representing different internal mechanisms. This begins with Identity, which is represented as the roots and main trunk of the tree which connects to all other parts of the tree.

The Root & Trunk = IDENTITY
The Branches = THOUGHTS which includes BELIEFS
The Leaves = EMOTION
The Flowers & Fruits = BEHAVIOURS & ACTIONS
The type and quality of the total Tree = OUR LIFE & REALITY

Identity is about who we define ourselves to be.
From identity comes thoughts, all thoughts belong to an internal "someone" also known as a "me".
Thoughts have a certain vibration, the quality of our thoughts can impact the kinds of emotions and actions we experience.

From thoughts, emotions are generated, this is represented as the foliage and leaves on the tree. Emotions are an output of energy in motion. This vibration can be felt and experienced.
You can't have emotions about things without there being some kind of thought process behind them because emotions are always about "something" and the only way that there can be a "something" is if the brain's attention is engaged to imagine, think about and perceive that "something".
Thoughts are the creators and drivers of emotion.

Actions are represented by the resulting flowers and fruits of the tree, they are the product and result of the identity, thoughts and emotions. This is what we sprout forth into the world.

Our total reality is represented by the state and quality of the entire tree.

Beliefs are like tools that can be picked up and dropped. Anyone can have one belief one day and then the opposite belief another day if they are willing to transform. When thoughts and emotions are put into action they become us and our reality which reflects who we are and what we say is true for us. This can be for better or worse, for detriment and limitation or for well-being and going beyond limitation.

This internal sequence determines the person's experience and quality of life, this can be the difference between a life that is like a damaged miserable weed with nothing but thorns, detrimental to other plants and/or a healthy blossoming fruit tree that is vibrant and healthy; to be a blessing and benefit to all.

Everyone is using this sequence one way or another and up until now, most of humanity has been operating this sequence to live an unconscious life and reality, where all of these steps of the sequence have contained detrimental things which are not preferred.
The same processes and mechanism is used to create any reality, be it from the darkest hells or to the brightest heavens. When we change these factors within ourselves then we alter and change the kind of plant we are and the kind of fruit and flowers that we produce and blossom into the world.

As we turn our attention inwards to recognise these things we become more consciously aware of what we are creating with our thoughts, words and actions.
If someone holds onto a detrimental identity of someone who is depressed and suicidal, then this is obviously going to impact all of the other parts of the tree, leading to depressed leaves and rotten fruit. It is the thoughts, emotions, and actions which lead people to having the experience of punishing themselves physically by "self harm", and the irreversible act of suicide itself.

This is why I emphasize the importance of looking at and addressing the internal identity, because identity is the first step. It is the root and source of all thoughts emotions behaviours and actions; and thus, our reality.

When we are consciously aware of who we define ourselves to be - how we define our world and reality; what we think, believe and say is true for us; become aware of our behaviours and actions, are able to view them all from a higher place; to understand the significance of those behaviours and actions and how they shape and create our reality - that's when our life can start operating on a whole other level. So much so, that I call this the "God level" and you will start to see and understand why as we progress throughout this series.

You have the power and ability right now to choose and make the decision for who you are going to be and what kind of life you are going to live. This requires us to consciously choose to take a moment of pause for ourselves - to calmly turn our attention to our breath, close our eyes and look inwards to question into the source of the thoughts we experience.

We become aware of how we may be limiting ourselves, limiting others or letting others limit us from blossoming into our full potential. We can then identify what needs changing and do what's needed to consciously create a new reality.

To look within ourselves with self-inquiry meditation is like going back to the original drawing board of reality with a blank canvas. When we are consciously aware of how our life and reality is created, then the choice for what kind of life and reality that we prefer to create is within our power - to choose a reality and life that is for the true well-being of all.

It is our responsibility and our choice about what kinds of thoughts, emotions and actions manifest into the world. The quality of our life on this world and beyond is in our hands. We can either make or break our existence. Life on earth can either be our heaven or it can be our hell, and whether or not you are aware of it or not, with every action we take we are choosing what kind of reality and world that we prefer.

Actions are to be used as tools for shaping and creating our reality. This is the true meaning of the expressions: "Be the change you want to see in the world". and "As you sow, so shall you reap". They are not just philosophical expressions.
They are hinting at a law of physics: cause and effect.

When you change your inner situation, then the outer situation follows suit and one shifts themselves to the reality where others are also being that vibration, for what we do internally is echoed externally. This is why state of being is so important if you want to make it to the higher vibrational realities.

I will discuss this more in depth throughout the series as it is also connected to much more advanced understandings that are extremely powerful and truly groundbreaking.

CHAPTER 9:

THE SUPERPOWER OF PRESENCE

Time is a created thing.
- Lao Tzu

"Mental Illness" can be defined in numerous ways. It all depends on who you ask and their definition of it. In my own lived experience I have found that the more truly awakened that we become, then the more we become aware of how mentally ill the vast majority of humanity really is. At the time of this books release, few are living a conscious and present life, society has been conditioned to live in ignorance and to live by many lies, one of those lies is regarding their concept of time.

Their concept of time has been a created delusion.

The mainstream brainwashed society and system had conditioned and taught the past detrimental self to unconsciously define itself and it's reality a certain way, with all sorts of beliefs, assumptions and limitations about itself and it's reality that were not true.

We don't have to go far to find unconscious and conditioned humans running on auto-pilot, for example when being served in shops or cafe's, some people would say things like *"sorry for the wait"*, or *"thanks for being patient"* but the fact of the matter is that there is no wait for one who is present and nor do we need patience, because we understand that everything is already here, that things are where they are meant to be and that there is nowhere else to be than in the present.

When one understands that the present is the most significant event happening, then what else is there to wait for?
Because all that is to come is more presence which is the same thing that is already here, the only difference is that the form of matter changes whereby the play of form can be seen from different points of view. However, it's always here and it's always now. When one's awareness is fully present then one has already arrived to the most significant place. This presence is the most true, real, and significant event happening.

It is one thing to understand this intellectually and an entirely different thing to understand this by direct lived experience. We have seen many people preaching this kind of awareness by social media, talking on podcasts or in front of crowds, but very few of them know what it means to live it.

I have lived this to the extreme of absolute pin point presence, whereby I came to see and understand that nothing moves, not only from the deeper "I" awareness, but because I understand that movement requires a past.
Where others would believe that the Sun comes up and goes down, rising and setting, I understood the deeper truth and awareness from my own observations. That the Sun does not move at all, not because the earth rotates around it but because it's always now.
In this awareness, regardless if it was sunrise or sunset made no difference, regardless if the entire galaxy and universe is dancing at an infinite range of speeds, that regardless if one is another being from another world or from a life lived millions of years ago, I knew that all unique viewpoints were seen from the same universal truth which is the here and now in this place of eternal presence.

As I gazed upon the perceived motion of sunrise, I could see the billions of still frames per second, yet aware that every frame is rooted in the same eternal presence.

Yesterday is history, tomorrow is a mystery, now is a gift; that's why it's called the present.

This is a well known saying that I'm sure many of you have come across and heard before, I have been unable to find the original source of it to be accredited to any one individual. It seems to be a saying that has gradually been added to by many people, developing and evolving from one generation to the next. None the less, what is most important is the message.

Ok, so what if the current reality we see sucks? That it isn't what we prefer? It may be something as simple as an untidy room.

It is very important to understand that your current situation is only the result of your past thoughts, emotions, behaviours and actions.

Look around your environment, whether you're in a room, a prison cell or a garden. Every placement of every single item in your environment, furniture, clothes, cups, pens, etc all have past thoughts, emotions, behaviours and actions behind them being there. Even if that means you sitting alone in nature by your choice to move yourself there, from the clothes you wear to the position that you stand or sit, all of it is the result of past thoughts emotions behaviours and actions.

In fact your very existence as this unique form that you are is also the result of your parents past thoughts emotions behaviours and actions, and on and on it goes to the very source of all creation.

The identity you have been which created the current situation that you see in your life and immediate reality doesn't have to be who you are right now.

IMAGE 3: TIME TO CHOOSE

Above: Image 3 – Time to Choose

You have the ability from this presence to choose to gradually transform yourself and your situation into just about anything.

Sadness, depression and suicidal characters arise when one is not present in the here and now. Where one may be connecting to a past self, identified with an old detrimental narrative and story, where things didn't work out. We recognise from this presence that yes, it may have been true for us in the past, but from now on in this presence we don't need to keep choosing to hold onto that detrimental identity or it's detrimental narrative and story.

> *If you are depressed, you are living in the past. If you are anxious you are living in the future. If you are at peace, you are living in the present.*
>
> - Lao Tzu

Being present with the here and now is naturally part of being well and having greater awareness, because how can anyone possibly feel afraid, anxious or depressed if they are truly present?

This presence is only ruined when people consume their presence with being "people", worrying about past and future which are both 100% non existential realities created in the mind.

Therefore the aim shouldn't be to first solve depression nor anxiety, but rather to first focus on cultivating more presence. This will naturally heal most depression and anxiety.

This presence is fundamentally uncorrupted. Only a busy and non present mind could possibly ever disturb this perfect presence.

Being in presence eliminates all suffering, and remember, for someone to be truly present, means that they are also without the conditioned, brainwashed and programmed identity, because that artificial identity is a formulation from the past.

If one is fully present then there is no past and no future, which also means there is no story or definition of *"how things are"*, or *"how the world is"* through the lens and viewpoint of the limited character identity.

Thus then, the story of "me" and the suicidal character identity construct also can't exist, because they require a past story to be identified with. A past story containing all sorts of beliefs and definitions about yourself and your reality, carried around with you like a big heavy sack of potatoes.

Presence is a powerful tool to let go of any baggage and lift us up onward to a major beneficial transformation.

So what if we made some mistakes in the past? We messed up, things got shitty. Perhaps we took a rough turn or lost everything, but so what?

When one is coming from the detrimental path and into a path of healing, one must understand that each rung on the ladder was part of the journey. Yes, some rungs on the ladder may have had their splinters, but they are there to teach us how to be stronger and show us better ways of doing things.
You are exactly where you need to be, every previous rung on the ladder, every person, place and thing, every scene, every single stepping stone that you took, led you to be here now hearing these words for a reason.
To have the opportunity to be free from that suffering and onto the path of transformation and growth towards a greater life of higher possibilities.

I'm even grateful now for all of the suffering I went through, for every rung on the ladder no matter how dark it was. Because I understand that it all contributed to my transformation and awakening that got me to where I am now.

Regardless of how dark and unpleasant the past may have been, it is by making this presence a great place to be, that we can find gratitude for all that came before it.

You can choose to create something completely different to all that was previously created. Only doubts and limiting thoughts and beliefs can say otherwise, and even with those doubts, limiting thoughts and beliefs, they only ever have as much power as we give them, it is our choice to choose whether or not we listen to them or rise above and beyond them.

Almost anything and everything is possible, the choice is in our hands right now with what we have, we can decide what will be true for us from this presence. We can choose to make it our heaven or our hell, we can make the choice and choose to change it right now for the better.

Because in this presence you are not defined.

This present moment and reality at it's core is not defined, the perceived outer world is not defined unless we choose for them to be, and how we choose to define them is out choice.

This presence is always a blank canvas for us to paint what we prefer, It is we who hold the paints and paintbrushes.

If you choose to believe that it's not a blank canvas and wish to continue the drama of the unconsciously created detrimental self i.e the conditioned programmed identity construct, then that is also what you are choosing to paint and create, which is a painting of doubt, detriment and limitation.

It is you who gives yourself and your reality definition and meaning and it is you who chooses and decides what is true for you regardless of what any so called "professional opinion" may be. It is you who are responsible to make the choice to own your life and take the wheel of your life into your own hands, to direct your life where you truly prefer. This understanding and analogy I discovered from within many years ago by my own direct experience and it is connected with how to cure labeled diagnosis which I will reveal to humanity in another book of this series.

I will now give you the direct answer and solution for you to take action on these 2 most effective way's that I know of in no particular order for increasing and cultivating a strong conscious presence in this life:

1. Time in nature, away from any technology, television, internet or things that have the artificial sense of time that most of society has been conditioned to live by. This includes isolating yourself away from other people who have been conditioned to live a life in unawareness of presence. Where one can be connected with the earth, have a camp fire, go for bush walks and sit with awareness of your surroundings, become a part of the natural environment and you will naturally re-align your awareness to what is most important. Nature always naturally shows us what is most important and that is what is happening right now.

2. Traditional Hatha Yoga as taught by Isha foundation where the breathing sequence is in harmony with the movements of the body. With practice, one comes to understand that nothing is more important than that breath, movement and position in that particular moment; rooting the awareness more and more into the present.

This awareness of conscious presence alone, can completely lift the veil and dissolve the fake reality that the mainstream media and fake system has sold to humanity.

CHAPTER 10:
THE STAGE OF LIFE - "ALL THE WORLD'S A STAGE"

Nothing de-programs conditioning and stops suffering better than the direct experience and awareness gained from internal action with self inquiry meditation. However, in order to begin that process we first need to create some distance between the character identity and who we truly are.

This creating of distance can greatly help in preparing for internal action. On my own journey this has resulted in a deeper, more encompassing and more profound understanding. It will make things easier with greater awareness, compassion, empathy and wisdom.

Suicide is "selfish" in the sense that what is left behind is deep and potentially life long pain for others. However, when I say that suicide is "selfish", I more importantly mean this with the deeper level of understanding, that there is a sense of "Self" that is responsible for it, the one who created that whole drama in the first place. It needs to be looked at, resolved and dissolved in order to be healed properly.

When I look back on my education from school, there was one single passage from William Shakespeare that stood out to me above everything else.

Throughout my journey I kept hearing it in my head, it has been immensely valuable in my own transformation towards recovery, healing and higher awareness. It was by far one of the most important things that was ever taught in school, and those words were:

"All the world's a stage,
And all the men and women merely players;
They have their exits and their entrances,
And one man in his time plays many parts"

As we contemplate this passage of Shakespeare, we come to see and realise that we have all worn many masks and played many characters throughout our lives. The vast majority of humanity live their life as a personality construct which from a true awakened level is recognised as an unconscious existence.

Throughout your life, you have been witness to the coming and going of many characters, acting out many emotions and behaviours. There have been many different emotional states written on your face as a result of the identity, it's thoughts and it's emotions.

There are many costumes and masks that you have worn, picked up and dropped on your journey of life. You know the happy one, the sad one, the loving one, the spiteful one, the caring one, the careless one, the depressed one, the empowered one, the hero, the villain, the victim. All of them different expressions of the multi-dimensional you, with different likes, dislikes and beliefs.

Both knowingly and unknowingly, consciously and unconsciously, all of those acts and masks of expressions have been played and worn by all of us, acting out our performance on the stage of life.

They come and go, like the autumn leaves that change colour, from yellow, to orange and then red. As they shed their leaves they are blown by the wind, landing upon the water, passing by as they float down the river stream and back to the earth.

So who are you that is the one who has been here the whole time watching and witnessing the coming and going? Who we really are is not a personality. Your personality identity is secondary to you.
By seeing the "me" from observer view and knowing that you have seen many "me's" come and go, then you know that you cannot be them. So, Who are we really? Let's see.

When learning about characters in the subject of drama, we will inevitably come across the word "persona".

A persona is a character, a way of acting and behaving, a personality construct, an artificial identity that was accumulated over time to form the psychological program of who you were taught to think you are and identify yourself with. A kind of fake costume that people are playing out as an act. Such identities are commonly referred to as a "me" which usually consists of a name that was given to us at birth, with an accumulated mental program consisting of likes, dislikes, preferences, opinions and beliefs, largely picked up from the outside world and our interactions with people.

Through truly awakened eyes we can see that anyone playing out an act via their unconsciously created personality construct is not only unconscious and un-awakened but also living a kind of lie.

Most humans prior to the release of this series, have been unconscious of the fact that they are living out an act, unaware that their life and reality can become just about any movie or play that they can imagine and create it to be.

This is not to say that those acts aren't genuine by any means, after all they are much of the life experience, they are what makes our life to be our diverse experience of life, however they are in most cases unconsciously lived, unaware that it's an act.

The core essence of you and who you really are, the eternal you is not a coming and a going through the revolving door like the numerous personality constructs you can play at being. The real you has been here all along watching the whole show.

You saw it all, starting with the name you were given. But names are just limited sounds, limited vibrations that we make with our mouths, they only become more than that when we give them meaning and identify ourselves with them, limiting ourselves with our own minds.

Would a rose smell as sweet by any other name?

If you have ever done acting in drama class and been given a different character name, or played a computer game and had to create a new character name, then it is very easy to understand that in most cases with rare exception, names are just made up and part of the limited artificial personality construct.

Listen to the following names like you are listening to them for the first time, like a sound being played from an instrument, and ask yourself what is an "Andrew"?, an "Alice"?, a "Ben"?, a "Julie", a "Robert", a "Maria", a "Joe"?, a "Sarah", a "Muhammad"?, a "Xi"?, a "Juan"?, a "Mike"?, a "Jenny"?, a "John"?

recognizing that they are just a sound.

A name is a limitation and reduction from all the sounds that we could possibly be, an unjust and poor representation of the magnitude of who we truly are. Although a name does serve it's purpose for participating in the play on the stage of life, in order to represent who we truly are, we would need to include every sound in existence, most of which are beyond the range of human senses. It is a word that cannot be spoken, an infinite sound that is already playing, thus there is no need to say it, because it is said without speaking.

This kind of awareness is connected to another topic regarding sound and vibration. Which also entwines into deeper understanding of spirituality and physics, such as the phrase "Nada Brahma" meaning "the universe is sound/vibration", with this understanding we can also come to recognise that there are no "swear words" or so called "hate speech" simply because they are only sounds. It is only the persons definition of those things, emotional investment into those things and lack of mental strength and resilience that causes them to be hurt by them.

Therefor, it is much more about that particular individual needing to do the inner work to not be affected by those things, rather than the entire society looking to go backwards and de-evolve to be controlled, limited and tied up in knots all because someone immature hasn't learnt the basics of mental and emotional resilience. Though I will be covering this and much deeper awareness of many things in other books of this series.

Which brings us back to the question: would a rose smell as sweet by any other name? The experience of a rose, all that it is and all of it's uses such as perfumes, deserts or a beautiful bunch of flowers given and received as a gift, is not fully experienced nor comprehended by only it's name.

Just as the name of a rose is a front cover to a world of sensory experience, names of humans are the front cover of an identity to a mental program consisting of thoughts, beliefs, opinions, likes, dislikes and preferences that shape one's entire experience of reality.

One can now recall those very early years when your name was given to you and repeatedly projected onto you. You were taught that the name is you, you picked it up, you identified with it, adopted it and accepted it as you, until over time you came to believe that it is you.
You owned that name, that sound you were given and identified with it to say *"yes ok then, that's me"*.
However, the truth is that it is not really you, because you are not your name, and nor do you have to be anything to do with it if you so choose. For some of course it may have some significance to you and it might serve you to maintain and hold onto it.

For many people that sense of self connected to their birth name has been unconsciously constructed to be something that they don't really prefer to be. Something much more limited to who and what they are capable of being. Where they are living a life that isn't really what they truly prefer to be living. Living life as a diminished sense of self as who they were taught to believe that they are, rather than being the fully fledged version of them that they were created to be. A sense of self that has been molded by others and constructed as a result of brainwashed conditioning with a diminished sense of self, lacking imagination for who and what one defines themselves, their life and reality to be. With doubts, conditioned beliefs and fears that only limit them and hold them back from who they really are and what they can become.

Personally I am using my given name for this book series because it is the name I had been given from birth which went through all that it did and overcame it. Until later on my spiritual journey it was no longer relevant as I'd gone beyond all names, though I have returned to it for now in order to finish this mission. It is suitable for my current needs because it represents a David vs Goliath situation in more ways than one, and so it's work is not quite done.

I also go by another name which is more of a spiritual name that was given to me using ancient methods of calculation, which I will consider revealing in an "about the author" section in an up and coming part of this series.

All thoughts and people who are outside are just characters in the play, but there is a way that we can remain above them all, not subject to the drama or game of unconsciousness that the vast majority of humanity have been playing.

Hidden messages for true awakening have been given to humanity, though I know that few have been aware of them and their significance. One of the most significant examples of this was in the popular TV hit series "Game of Thrones" where in Season 6 episode 2, a much deeper awareness and truth, intentional or not, was revealed by the creators. If you haven't seen the scene that I will be referring to, I suggest that after reading this, that you go and find it on YouTube or another media platform to see it for yourself.

The most significant scene that I am referring to in particular, involved the characters Arya Stark and Jaqen H'ghar.
Arya had been outcast from the temple of the faceless ones, she had gone blind and was homeless, begging on the streets of the city of Bravos.
She was then confronted by the other faceless disciple, who asked her who she was, beating her up with a stick as they tested her.

Arya became overwhelmed before she was then confronted by Jaqen H'ghar;

Jaqen said: "Who are you?"

Arya replied: "No one.."

Jaqen continued: "If a girl say's her name, A man will let her sleep under a roof tonight."

Arya replied: "A girl has no name."

Jaqen: "If a girl say's her name, a man will feed her tonight."

Arya: "A girl has no name."

Jaqen: "If a girl say's her name, a man will give her eye's back."

Arya: "A girl has no name."

Jaqen: "Come."

Arya then reaches for her beggar's bowl, but Jaqen stops her in her tracks with one of the most significant lines in the whole series saying: **"Leave it, a girl is not a beggar anymore."**

In that moment with Jaqen's guidance, Arya instantly leaves the beggar identity behind.

The reason that this scene is so significant and powerful for humanity to understand is that in real life this can happen just as easily in the same way. That it really is that easy to drop a detrimental identity that is leading us down a path and life that we don't prefer. I have often heard people unconsciously say things like "people don't change" but that is just a conditioned/brainwashed limiting belief system that acts as a road block to change. Once that belief system is removed, then one has every possibility to change. Limiting beliefs and doubts are only temporary road blocks and limitations standing in the way of one from realising their freedom and higher potential.

Overcoming suicidal thoughts and behaviours and mental illness in general is largely about shifting our point of view to rise above and see ourselves, our situation and our life story from a different, higher and more evolved perspective.

To see that all of those negative things that we kept buying into about ourselves and kept telling ourselves and believing about ourselves, weren't fundamentally true. It is only that by listening to them and believing in them, that they may have been true for us temporarily while we were buying into that identity of ourselves and playing that character. That character only survived off the energy and attention that we fed it. The detrimental self is maintained by the identification with it, this is one of the reasons why diagnosed labels only prolongs illness.

Every voice and opinion belongs to a "someone", a character on the stage of life.

If you want to overcome the suffering of the personality identity construct then you need to recognise that you are not your thoughts, and that you are not this detrimental character creating the drama, the detrimental story of "me", because you can be witness to it.

Let's take a look now at the following image called "Image 4 The Stage of Life" it's purpose is to help in visually understanding and comprehending the following concept.

We will now do a short little exercise together to put things into perspective. See, imagine and visualize yourself now, as though you are in a theater. View that detrimental character that you have been playing and experiencing like it is an actor on the stage external to you. Seeing yourself in the audience now, watching the drama on the stage. You can see all the actors and actresses, the characters of the play. You can see and witness that suicidal character, now looking at it from a distance as it acts out it's little dramatic performance on the stage.

You are not affected by it, because you know that you are in the audience and that it's just a play.

IMAGE 4: THE STAGE OF LIFE

Above: Image 4: "The Stage of Life"

Imagine that character with a speech bubble saying "I'm not good enough", you can see that character from an observational perspective looking down upon them from the position of the audience at a distance, unattached to any emotion of it.

You can envision any internal thought as a cartoon character in a scene, playing their part, with a speech bubble saying that thing, that line, that script and narrative, the purpose of this is to turn that statement into an actor or actress. If they are a detrimental character that you need to overcome and dissolve, then you can see everything they say and think as nothing more than like a character in a comic book with a speech bubble, recognizing that anything which could potentially be written into a speech bubble coming from the mouth of a character or person, can be overcome and observed from a place of deeper awareness.

This is not about denial or ignoring and hiding your darkness but rather, this is about stepping back from that sense of "self" character, taking yourself out of the fog to see more clearly.

Because when you visualize yourself in the position of the audience, watching and seeing that detrimental self or suicidal character version of yourself on the stage, you are no longer controlled by it, by not associating yourself with them, you become unaffected by their drama.

We come to see that all of its beliefs, statements, despair, fear, anxiety, guilt, shame, depression, victimization, the one who is ill, with problem X,Y and Z, all of it's hardships and baggage can now be at a distance from you.

For example, when we observe the statement of "I'm not good enough", coming from that character we know that such a statement is coming from someone who feels sad, down, and depressed. They have a frown, with sad eyes, they are clearly unhappy.

See them sitting on a chair looking down and burying their face into their hands in utter misery, acting out their little drama like an actor or actress in a play. Recognise that the narrative and script of "I'm not good enough" belongs only to that character.

As you contemplate your new position in the audience,
you can recognise that the unconsciously created sense of "me" as the depressed and/or suicidal character, with all of its problems and all of it's drama on the stage of your life doesn't have to be yours any longer. You can allow yourself to step back from it now and say: "Hey, I don't have to be that act any more".

When you can see this character from a distance, then who are you to be looking at it from this distance? Clearly that sense of "me" character is not you because you are now the one who is being a witness to it. You can see and witness them, aware that they are no longer you.

The only way that they can be you, is if you CHOOSE to let them be. It is your choice if it serves you to keep wearing those outfits and playing those acts, for you are responsible for your own life.

When you choose to let go of the detrimental characters that you were being, then all of those character's problems, dramas and baggage can go with them because it's no longer yours to carry.

Forgive your "self"

Forgiveness is a beneficial mechanism to understand and apply internally, this is relevant to all of humanity which starts first and foremost within us. When you apply forgiveness internally to the many internal selves, then this also greatly contributes in lighting the way to internal liberation.

Because when you can have compassion, empathy, understanding and forgiveness for your own life and story of the past, then you will also naturally have that for all people who are playing out those characters and expressions that you have experienced.

"**Don't be dead serious about life, it's just a play**"
- Sadhguru

When we apply this understanding to the suicidal character, we can recognise that when that suicidal character has said it's lines and played it's part in our play, that it no longer needs to take the spotlight and no longer needs to occupy the stage of our mind and our life. The story we live is no longer about them, the suicidal character is no longer relevant or needed in our story and inevitably that suicidal character becomes nothing more than an act of the past.

You only chose to wear the mask, forgetting that you were wearing one at all, as has most of humanity, playing dress ups in the business suits and so forth. Everyone is playing characters, but those characters aren't who we really are. Overcoming the suicidal character in this way is like being the director of your own play, where you are choosing to fire that actor from your play. If you are the director in charge of your own play in life, then you can decide what your play through life will be. This is not at all meant to de-value the experience of the story and the experience of the personality constructs, for they all had their purposes and played their parts.

This is to bring greater awareness to let you know that you have a choice for who you wish to be and how you wish your life to be.
The director is responsible for the performance, when you take responsibility as the director in charge of your own life and performance, only then can you have the ability to direct your own life and correct your own performance.

Don't let others dictate and determine what is true for you, it is you who have the choice and power to decide right now in this presence for what will be true for you.

Make the decision to be your own director, your own master, starting with writing your own script and narrative for your own life and what you wish it to be.

The more aware we become of our acts on the stage of life, the more we are able to change and re-design our character and life into the one that we most truly prefer. In order to do this, we first need to re-direct our attention and focus away from what was previously created, away from other people, away from the noise of television and other pixels and other distractions, taking some time out for ourselves to turn our attention inwards.

Go back to the blank canvas and redesign yourself and your life for what you truly wish it to be, think about that version of you, what is that version's characteristics? What does their sleeping pattern look like?, What do they eat? How fit and healthy are they? How do they speak? What do they wear? Who is in their company? How do they treat other humans and other life? What do they do? How much money do they have coming in? What does their life and reality look like? What impact does this version of you have on the whole? Once you know this, then start taking the steps to make that your reality.

CHAPTER 11:
THE SECRET OF THE WORDS - "I WANT TO KILL MYSELF"

"If one is not afraid of going to sleep, I don't see why one should be afraid of killing the mind or ego by Sadhana"
- Sri Ramana Maharshi (Sadhana means spiritual practice, in this instance Self Inquiry)

Some people are afraid of losing their character, but character is just a mask we hold, and fear of losing it is yet another one. If you never drop them, then you forget who the real you is, in fact you don't even experience the real you. Because the real you is beyond character or name, it is the one who has been holding all of the characters up all this time from the very beginning.

A person who is contemplating suicide is seeking a way to end their suffering, and that suffering always belongs to an identity construct. In order to overcome and cure suicidal thoughts emotions and behaviours completely, you need the awareness that the suicidal character itself acting out it's drama, is just another character that we have played or experienced on the stage of life.

Anyone who experiences suicidal thoughts, emotions and self harming behaviours will always come across the thought of something along the lines of *"I want to kill myself"*, because these are the words of the script that belongs to that character, along with a range of other thoughts as to why such a statement might be justified. If you've come to this point within yourself, where you have heard the words along the lines of *"I want to kill myself"* within you, then firstly I'd like to congratulate you, because you are actually far closer to liberation from suffering and closer to true awakening than most people may ever be in their lifetime.

This is because if we hear the words *"I want to kill myself"* in our head, we discover the great irony that we are also giving ourselves the answer and solution to overcome it. In other words, the solution to overcoming Suicide is given in this statement of - *"I want to kill myself"*.

The important thing to understand here is that our suicidal sense of "self" character identity construct is precisely what we need to "kill" and transform in order for us to overcome it and allow ourselves to live our best life.

To ensure that there is no misunderstanding to anyone reading this, I don't at all mean killing in terms of taking the irreversible and final action of death by leaving the body. This is not about leaving the body, suicide by leaving the body is not the solution. In order to end suffering and live on with a good quality of life, the person who is suffering needs to look inwards at the source of the suffering to confront it and solve it from within. When I speak about killing your *"self"* it is simply a metaphor to describe the dissolvement of that detrimental identity construct of *"the one who is suicidal"*.

That's the one that needs to be investigated and that's the one that needs to *"die"*, not you. It's about dissolving the story of the *"me"* who is feeling suicidal saying those detrimental things, by questioning, inquiring into them when they arise, and seeing that character and all of their little dramas and issues from a higher place of observation, to recognise that it's not you, that the character was picked up, accumulated, and formed over time.

This is the true meaning of the well known wise words - *"THE ONLY WAY OUT, IS IN."*

By taking a step inwards to look at the source of our thoughts and emotions using self inquiry meditation, we can confront them and put the flames of those negative suicidal thoughts and emotions to rest by recognizing and questioning the sense of "self" that is suggesting and saying those things to begin with, stopping them in their tracks before it becomes a great depression or worse; the irreversible action of suicide.

This is why killing my unconscious and conditioned sense of "self" by Self Inquiry meditation was one of the best things that I ever did, and I would highly recommend that the whole of humanity needs to be doing it.
In fact, it is the best thing that you can possibly do for your mental health.
It enables us to break through the many conditioned limitations of reality because all limitations and mental illness in general, or anything unpleasant at all belongs to a *"someone"*, a sense of *"self"*, that can be internally dissolved with Self Inquiry Meditation.

We can also recognise that the words *"I want to kill myself"* reveals the illusion of there being more than one person here, it implies that there are two people within you, the "I" and the *"self"*. If you kill the self, then it means that you're still here. Once again giving yourself the answer, because the "I" is the real you which is saying that it wants to destroy the fake self.

Look at these words, what is *"MY-SELF"*? clearly It has to be an addition to you and when you recognise that it's not you, then you won't need to carry it around with you.

If you have seriously contemplated suicide, then it means that you have been willing to let go of the whole story of the unconsciously programmed, and constructed sense of *"self"*. If one knows that it was all a disaster, then one is more easily able to let go of it, like letting go of a pair of well worn smelly socks with holes in them that you don't need. It's much easier to let go of the old life and to internally do a reset like a blank canvas, to re-imagine, re-design and re-choose your life. To make a conscious decision about who you are going to be and what you want your life to be, rather than what others think you are and say you are.

It is useful to think of suicide as something that doesn't belong to anybody. It is just a character that some people move through during their life, and so it's not really anybody's to carry, in fact, it really isn't.

Suicidal personas, i.e characters, are only sustained by the identification with them. The identification with that diminished, depressed, limited and negatively oriented *"story of me"* that is in suffering.

When a thought that is depressive, suicidal or in despair arises in the mind, there's always a reason. It's always about a little story of *"me"*, which say's like *"oh I am this way because X Y Z is happening"*, *"XYZ always happens"*, *"XYZ is the way it is"*, where that identity defines reality saying that "things are this way" to try and justify all the reasons why you should feel bad.

However, they are only thoughts and beliefs, they are only opinions, and they can only become real by you agreeing that they are true and real for you by buying into them as true, remember, as you sow, so shall you reap.

The detrimental *"story of me"* needs to be let go of to be fully present and awakened. It belongs to the past, and by letting it go you are not losing anything, it can still be a valuable memory that you learnt from, but you don't need to carry your story as a detrimental baggage nor let it dictate who you are in the present.

Because ultimately, the suicidal character is the product of thoughts and beliefs, which means that whole drama can also just as easily be transformed and let go of completely because we can transform and let go of our thoughts and beliefs easily and completely.

IMAGE 5: NO MORE BAGGAGE

Above: Image 5: No More Baggage

That whole story belongs to the past, which has no power over the present unless you choose to say that it does, and if you do, then recognise that you are choosing that from the present.

You can now see that the depressed and suicidal character and story was created, picked up and accumulated along your journey of life. That the only power that it ever has is the power that you choose to give it, by buying into it, believing it, investing your energy into it by making it your thing to carry, your narrative, your identity and your story.
But now you can choose to let it all go if you really want to, because you can simply recognise that it no longer serves you.

"When you are no longer interested in what the mind has to sell you, it is done, it is finished, suffering is no longer a thing in your life"
- Mooji

Identity is the key, the source and the root of all internal suffering, because all suffering has to belong to a *"someone"*.
When we can turn our attention inwards to overcome and disassociate from that *"someone"*, then there is no-one there within us who is suffering.

Solidify your new reality in the present, as the one who has now let go of the suffering of the past, because if we are always going back into the past and dwelling on the drama, problems, struggle and baggage of the past, then it is like sifting through an old rubbish bag. You would only do that if you had left something in that rubbish bag that was extremely valuable that serves you well for the path ahead.

If you are currently experiencing suicidal thoughts such as *"I want to kill myself"* then you can also replace the word *"kill"* with the word *"overcome"*. Listen to what that sounds like and feels like now, how this shifts things internally, because now the new voice says *"I want to overcome myself"*. One then starts to see *"hey wait... who am I then to overcome that "self"?*, revealing the truth that it's not you.

You can recognise that it's not really you, that it was formulated and picked up along the way, this isn't about denial and nor is it about believing it's not you, it's about KNOWING it's not you by your own clear direct experience of observation and being witness to the dissolvement of the conditioned and fake sense of self.

I feel that it's also worth mentioning here that the approach of the mental health system has long stood in the way of progress and wellness.
For example, when it comes to disassociation, they don't fully understand nor support the need for disassociation from suffering let alone the detrimental identity. That often when someone first arrives, they would be asked to fill out a number of forms and answer many questions.
Some of those questions ask how much the person disassociates themselves from unpleasant feelings, identity and people. Implying that there is something wrong with them if they do, making it out to be some kind of illness or so called "disorder" if they are someone

who disassociates themselves from these things which couldn't be further from the truth.

As I have pointed out many times in this book, disassociating from that detrimental identity is crucial to overcoming it. It is the same thing for example if we wanted to overcome drugs, then we wouldn't associate our self and put our self in a drug filled environment surrounded by junkies. The act of labeling someone as being ill, just for choosing not to associate with that detrimental sense of self identity and it's drama, shows an incredible lack of understanding by the mainstream mental health system. It's like bullying and punishing someone for making a healthy decision.

So don't let your identity be associated with and occupied with the suicidal character or any other unhelpful and detrimental characters for that matter, even addictions can be overcome with the application of this knowledge.

If you have come this far, having read everything up to this point, then you are now ready for the next chapter where we will be diving into Self Inquiry Meditation, which is one of the main key components needed to permanently overcome suicide and also mental illness in general.

CHAPTER 12:
THE POWER OF SELF INQUIRY MEDITATION – "WHO AM I?"

"realization of the self is the greatest help that can be rendered to humanity."
- Sri Ramana Maharshi

"I Am is the name of God. Of all the definitions of God, none is indeed so well put as the Biblical statement "I Am that I

Am" in Exodus (chap. 3). There are other statements, such as Brahmaivaham, Aham Brahmasmi, and Soham. But none is so direct as the name Jehovah = I Am. The Absolute Being is what is – it is the Self. It is God. Knowing the Self, God is known. In fact, God is none other than the Self."
— Ramana Maharshi, Talks With Ramana Maharshi: On Realizing Abiding Peace and Happiness (p. 76)

In this chapter we will dive into Self-Inquiry and bring everything that we have covered full circle. I will also be using the word "God" and I know that this can be a sensitive and tricky word to use and navigate in literature especially when so many people all over the world have varying belief systems and definitions of such a word.

However I do deeply understand this which goes beyond belief systems and have found the way of truth by which even atheists and believers can be correct at the same time which involves going deeper.

This deeper knowledge I will reveal bit by bit throughout this series which when understood has the capacity to unite all of Humanity in the deepest truth.

"Truth is one, paths are many"
- Mahatma Gandhi

> *"The way of truth is like a great road. It is not difficult to know it. The evil is only that men will not seek it."*
> \- Mencius (Mengzi)

If you aren't interested in knowing the truth within you and want to continue the lie to yourself then you are not ready for Self Inquiry.

If you are interested in truth, then by all means please continue.

There have been many other so called "meditations" which are built only on fantasy and delusion, causing the person to be entranced by the thinking and imagining mind as they focus on the soft fluffy pink clouds, which at best is only a temporary peaceful distraction without any true and lasting beneficial outcome.

Any meditation that doesn't first and foremost investigate and dissolve the source identity of the drama to go beyond it and the thinking mind is a mediocre form of meditation. The popular trend of "mindfulness meditation", although temporarily beneficial for some, it is not designed to bring true awakening, it is only about creating temporary states of feeling ok, dancing around the edges of true awakening, because it doesn't address the identity at it's core root. It keeps the person within the boundaries of the identity construct focusing on its output of feelings rather than the source of the feelings.

If I am to be directly blunt with you, then I would say that all characters are a kind of lie, a mask, a construct, a fleeting creation that has a beginning and an end, however, who we truly are is a deeper awareness beyond them, which is eternal, undying, you could call it "God" or "Shiva" which literally translates to "that which is not", an awareness which allows both atheists and believers of God to both be right at the same time.

I am one who has solved many of these bigger questions and long standing mysteries for humanity, not just intellectually, I have lived it, this isn't a belief system, I haven't come to this understanding by believing in something, I KNOW it, by direct lived experience of deeper truth.

However many people won't be ready for this degree of directness, and I know that it raises many resistances in conditioned minds, especially those bound by distorted religious indoctrination with many questions, I am aware of what those questions are, all of which I will answer throughout this series to bring the whole of humanity together in awareness and understanding of deeper truth.

In order to address the weeds of the mind, to overcome suicide and mental illness in general, then just like any good gardener with the task of pulling weeds out from their garden, we must also approach mental illness and suicide in the same way, which means removing them by the root! So what is the root?

The root is Identity. Essentially, by clearing the false identity, self inquiry enables the inquirer a clear path back to the source of their existence which is found in the heart. Identity is the only thing standing in the way between the mind and the heart. Once the ego identity of the "me" is removed, then the god-self identity of "I" remains.

The "I" that is without identity is the root of all, which is found in the heart.

There is no mistake about such phrases as "home is where the heart is" hinting at a much deeper understanding of the way to God residing in the heart. This is also why Jesus is often depicted as pointing towards his heart and the well known quote from the bible reminds it's readers "The kingdom of heaven is found within you".

This is also seen with the sequence of formation in the womb, where we see the first part of the human to form is the heart. In the sacred geometric seed of life pattern.

This will be of utmost importance for our humanity in coming decades to make the conscious choice to turn our focus, attention and awareness back to our hearts. I will discuss these topics in greater depth in up and coming parts of this series.

Understanding and practicing Self Inquiry meditation has real psychological and spiritual significance and benefit. Which when it is understood; has the ability to liberate us from noisy minds of suffering and onward into clarity, wisdom, and inner peace. Unlocking a whole new level of higher awareness and well-being.

So what is self Inquiry?
Some people would spell this as "Self Enquiry" with an E, though I choose to spell it with an "I" written as "Self IN-quiry". The reason for this is because it emphasizes the fact that it is about going INwards to question and Inquire within.
Self Inquiry has existed for as long as there have been humans to question their own minds. However this practice was made more well known by the Indian sage born under the name Venkataraman Iyer, better known as Bhagavan Sri Ramana Maharshi.

Self-inquiry is not a difficult practice. Its actually very easy, perhaps the easiest and also the most true and powerful form of meditation that one can experience.
It is one of the key things that contributed to my ability for overcoming and curing not only moderate forms of mental illness such as anxiety and depression, but also more severe forms of mental illness such as

suicidal thoughts, emotions, behaviours and even diagnosed mental illness such as "Schizoaffective disorder".

From my lived experience, Self Inquiry Meditation is the best tool you could possibly use to deep clean your mind. It can and will work for anyone who applies it, simply because everyone's core root source is "I".

Self Inquiry is a way by which we can remove the internal obstacles, it can and will help you to recognise that the one suggesting those ideas and thoughts of suicide and all other negative things about yourself and your reality is not you, and in fact it never was, because you will come to see and realise that who you really are is not your mind.

It shows us and proves that our name, identity constructs, their thoughts and their beliefs are not who we truly are, that they are more like temporary tools that we pick up and borrow.

Self Inquiry cleans away all that is not yours to carry clearing the path towards clarity, awareness, lasting well-being, enlightenment and spiritual advancement as a whole, healing all that is unhealed hurt and broken within. It is the best way that I know of for anyone to reveal the truth of their own psychologically programmed conditioning and the deeper truth of all.

It is a process of honest introspection, of internal investigation, of sincere truth seeking and ultimately truth discovery.
Which is why it will work most effectively when approached with sincerity to know the truth.

Self Inquiry is a destroyer of ignorance and falseness.
It allows one to see who they truly are by the direct experience of the deeper "I" (the God-self) that is within us all.

Discovering the identity through emotion.

If we reflect on what was outlined in the important earlier chapter called "The Sequence Tree". Then we know that when we are feeling emotions, we can trace those emotions back to specific thoughts that generated them and back towards the root internal source character identity saying and thinking that thing.

Remember that emotions were represented in our sequence tree as the leaves. In the same way that we can identify plants by their leaves, the emotion is the hint, the clue as to identify what the thought is and the kind of character that the thought and emotion would belong to.

So, if you are not sure about the thoughts and identity that are causing your unpleasant emotional state of being, then first feel what the emotion is that you are feeling. Once you identify the emotion and feeling that you feel, you can then identify the kind of character identity that is behind it. We can see what they would be thinking in order to feel that way. You can then figure out what the identity is that those thoughts belong to.

Pause and ask yourself for a moment: Who is the character saying and believing those things? What kind of character would say or believe such a thing?, What do they look like if you were to see an image of them?

For example if the emotion is sadness then it is
"The sad one" character. So we internally ask, to whom has this sorrow arisen? Essentially, it is *"the one who is carrying the sad story"* and thus being the character that is sad. In the practice of doing this and revealing this to yourself the reason for sadness may also be revealed.

It's also worth mentioning that

If one is being the sad character or any other character in that moment then it excludes all other possibility of being a different character in that moment.

Only 1 person (persona) can occupy the cubicle at a time.

The cubicle of *"self"* is occupied and engaged with being that character and it's state of being.

Recognizing that once your cubicle in the mind is free from being occupied with that identity character, then only then is there any possibility of you being vacant and available to being any character and state of being that you prefer.

There isn't anything wrong with feeling sadness or any other emotion, by all means feel it and work through it internally if you wish, as this can be a healing process in and of itself. I often found on my own journey that my sadness left with my tears and so tears were a way to heal. Though just know that you don't need to stay there and dwell in the sadness if you don't want to.

If one can see this one that is sad from a distance then the one looking at the one who is sad cannot be the one who is sad, because the reasons for being sad belongs to that sense of self character identity acting out the sadness.

Once you can see that character responsible for that thought, you can ask yourself sincerely along the lines of *"well if I can see them, then who am I?"* One then disintegrates that *"me"* and moves more strongly into the "I".

There is no emotion of hate or anger or anything else as you dissolve the identities, there is only recognition and awareness of them, there is an awareness that those characters are just another part of creation that contributes to the infinite expressions of all. Your perspective of them can be neutral without emotion.

It can be important that you can see their points of view and expression as valid without labeling and judging them as bad and negative or anything else.

Have no judgment of the many selves that you come across and witness within you, because we all contain them all and they all have their place and purpose on the stage of life. Be aware that if you judge them then you are taking on the identity of a judger which must also be dissolved if you want to go all the way.

As you dissolve these things for example with the judger, you can then become non-judgemental to others, in this way, each dissolvement is like gaining an additional superpower which grows into greater super powers such as being able to not make assumptions about anyone or anything.

As you dissolve the identity constructs of many selves forgiving those selves, you can naturally have understanding and compassion for them, unattached emotionally, yet in gratitude for it's teaching, knowing that it was a temporary character and a mask which served a purpose for its time.

Empathy, Compassion and Non-judgement can also come about by recognizing that we are not our thoughts, that the way people think and what they believe in and buy into is not who they really are. It's fundamentally just sparks of neurons firing off in their brains, thoughts that they are grabbing at. Much of the time they do this unconsciously and so it is easy to have compassion for them.

Beliefs are like tools that can be picked up and dropped. Anyone can have one belief one day and then the opposite beliefs another day if they are willing to transform.

One of the great things about this process of self inquiry, is also that when one opens their eyes and decides to engage with the outer world and looks upon other people, then one begins to have compassion for all of humanity and all of the characters on the stage of life, knowing that 99% of people have unconsciously bought into beliefs and programs that they just don't realise is not them, limiting themselves to be a particular character.

One can look to others without judgement knowing all too well that every facial expression is the result of a neurological circuit making a spark in their brain.

When we have explored sufficiently inward to know about our own emotions and faces and the thoughts associated to them, then it becomes easier to also see, feel and know the thoughts of others.

You can even begin to know exactly what is on someone's mind. Such power is only given because one has compassion and understanding of all the other characters within their own being.

On my own journey I have experienced being able to read people and know what's going on within them better than they even know themselves. Every facial position is the result of thoughts and one's sense of identity, for what one is feeling and thinking can be read in the face, the eyes, and felt vibrationally. When the emotions behind the face are known, then so are the thoughts and beliefs.

> **"Your nature is Peace and Happiness. Thoughts are the obstacles to realization. A thought must be quelled as soon as it rises. Whenever a thought arises, do not be carried away by it."**
> - Sri Ramana Maharshi

The process of Self Inquiry involves internally inquiring, questioning and asking into the thought that arises within us.

This can be any internal thought, voice, belief or opinion that may arise. Essentially you are seeking the source of it, the root character identity behind the thought and asking "Who am I?".

The "I" awareness is deeper, and transcendental to all points of view and all senses of anyone's "me" with a view or opinion.

Listen to the statement or belief that the identity is stating, saying and suggesting. As each thought arises, we simply ask it "to whom has this thought arisen?" or "who's thought is this?"
The answer will either be complete silence or the identity construct will reveal itself to say "me". If you can see that "me" at a distance from you then you ask "Who am I?" upon which the "me" is seen as the false sense of self, disintegrated as you move closer into the "I" of who you truly are.

While practicing Self-Inquiry, your Sincerity is a very sharp and powerful tool, when your question of "who am I?" is armed with the power of sincerity, you will be able to cut through and burn through the toughest cobwebs of illusion to discover and realise the God-self within you.
So the question remains "who am I?" to come to a point in yourself where you are ready to sincerely investigate this within, not just as a procedure, but to sincerely be asking this to yourself because you recognise that you sincerely don't know who you are, then this is a big milestone achievement.

When questioning the artificial personality constructs and detrimental thoughts of the mind with "who am I?", the sincerity in the question literally sears it, it disintegrates it and burns it up. This rings true of the words "the truth shall set you free" and can never be more true when applied internally.

Bit by bit, emotion by emotion, thought by thought, little "me" by little "me", one begins to clear and de-program the conditioned mind's thinking, where one begins to see the world with the new vision of truth and deeper awareness.

Continue applying this approach of self-inquiry to all thoughts within, you may discover many within you that you were not even aware of. The following are some more examples of personality/character constructs that are dissolved with Self Inquiry to realise the God sense of "I" within.

Continue to see if you have any of the following character identities within you that you are holding onto, that you may be running your energy through, unconsciously identified with and thinking that they are you. The less you have of them, the more advanced and enlightened you will become. Ask these questions internally.

Who is doubting?, Who is early?, Who is late?, Who is rushing?, Who is delayed?, Who is urgent?, Who is angry?, Who is unhappy?, Who is sad?, Who is lonely?, Who is judging?, Who is defining?, Who is trying?, Who is ill? Who is analyzing?, Who is aging?, Who dies?

You don't necessarily have to hunt those identities, you can just dissolve them as they arise with "who am I?".
Who is asking?, Who asked that?, And this?, Who is the questioner?, Who remains?
I, I, I... until only "I" remains.

As you recognise that those identities aren't you, the false characters are dissolved one by one as you hold that space of the deeper "I".

This is a place of effortlessness, of not reaching for thoughts, a place of non-doing. This is the "God-self", it is one thing to intellectually understand it and a completely different thing to experientially know it, I am one who knows it.

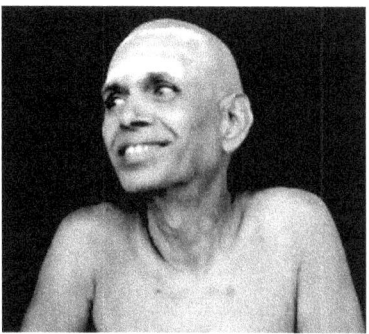

"You must become nothing, only a person who is nobody can abide in the self (God)"
- Sri Ramana Maharshi

So who am I? This question itself is then seen – who is asking? And who is asking about who is asking? Meaning that the question in and of itself to be asking "who is asking?"; is the same identity. Which of course is the Questioner. When you realise this, then you will see that the remaining identity is the identity of a Questioner, asking this question "who am I?".

This is the only character left, the one that you had deployed from the beginning; the questioner who is seeking truth. You can imagine that character in your mind questioning everything, asking questions is it's primary character function. Obviously they are someone who wants to know something, otherwise there wouldn´t be a question, therefore we can recognise that they are the identity of "the one who doesn't know".

Circling back to my cubicle analogy now, we can recognise that for one to be the identity of one who is searching and questioning, as *"the one who doesn't know"*, then it means that one is occupied with that, by being occupied with *"the one who doesn't know"*, then one stops them self from being *"the one who knows"*. Therefore they cannot pass to the ultimate "I" and be the one where the search is over because they are busy being occupied with the one who is searching with the question "Who am I?".

When this one is also dissolved and disintegrated, and only the "I" remains. It is then, that without question one knows they are "God"(I), one knows the truth of things, that all are "God"(I), there is no separation for there is no-one else to be, beyond identity, opinions and characters, one goes beyond dualism, transcendental to all views and perspectives not subject to them but can see them all, it is the "I"(eye) behind and beyond all eyes (viewpoints/beliefs/opinions/characters).

Essentially this has the power to stop all mental illness because any statement, opinion or reason for anyone stopping you from being well and cured can also be disintegrated and dissolved. Any statement is responded with *"oh is that so? say's who? Who is this character? Who am I?"*. All identities and characters become irrelevant and inferior to the God-self awareness. You burn them in the deepest of truths from the eye of God within you.

The God-self within all of us is transcendental to all emotions, pain and suffering and we can all access that through the process of self-inquiry. It is well known and considered by many yogis, mystics and sages throughout the ages as the most direct way to know God and truth.

From my direct experience, I have come to understand that this dissolvement or what I prefer to call disintegration process is the same thing which is known as the burning eye of Shiva. This is what I have seen within my own process my eye (as Shiva) disintegrating those identities and we all have this ability within us, because we are all God.

Without any harm there is a beautiful internal destruction and disintegration of the detrimental selves, freeing and liberating us from all that is holding us back from being who we truly are and living a happy and wonderful life, reclaiming our divine birthright as truly awakened and truly enlightened beings.

CHAPTER 13:
POTENTIAL RESISTANCES AND IMPEDIMENTS TO SELF INQUIRY MEDITATION

"There are no impediments to meditation, the very thought of such obstacles is the greatest impediment."
- Sri Ramana Maharshi

During the process of self inquiry, we may have a very busy mind saying *"I can't, it's too hard"*, THESE are the voices and characters to question into and look at who they are, which is the doubter, the defeatist, the one having a tantrum, who gives up, and limits themselves.

In particular listen out for any voices of limitation that say *"I can't"* followed by the thing that it believes it can't.

Any such statements within you are red flags, because all of those expressions are roadblocks. Such a statement belongs to a character of limitation, who views this as a big thing and something that is a struggle and difficult.

While ever you hold onto them and believe in them they will only block and limit you to stop you from growing.

When I would speak to people about being present or overcoming the noise of the mind they would often say *"but it's hard!"* I would say "Say's who?"

There was an experience that I had where I was wearing a shirt which said "Disobey" on the front of it and a woman asked me what I was disobeying. I replied "thoughts of the mind". She said *"oh.. but that's hard"*. I said "Well, that's a thought isn't it?" after a moment she comprehended the depth and significance of what I was saying and said *"Thank you!"*.

If you find with this process yet another self panicking or worrying about things or doubting, then inquire into that one too with the same process. If there is another self saying that *"this is hard"* or *"I don't get this"* then apply the same process.

Inquire into those characters and see them. What characters are they playing and what do they look like? Who am I?

Every thought and feeling of emotion belongs to a *"someone"*, the more that you practice this process, the easier it becomes and the visualization of the internal characters will come to you instantly.

Those voices of limitation and doubt have no more power than what we choose to give them. We can also flip the switch on them, because the opposite voice to *"I can't. It's too hard, It doesn't work for me"*, is "I can, it's easy, and it does work for me, because it's worked for others and there is no reason why it can't work for me too". Any other reason not to succeed that may come up within you can also be questioned and dissolved from the question "Who am I?". Those limitations are only voices and opinions that you can simply choose not to buy into or allow them to limit you or hold you back; they are automatically dissolved from the awareness of the "I".

While ever there is a single negative or limiting belief system then there also exists the opposite belief system of something unlimited and positive. All opinions and beliefs exist. The one that you choose to hold is up to you.

Remember, belief systems are simply tools for shaping and sculpting reality, so on this level of awareness, we become aware that it's a matter of choice for what we choose to believe and decide is true for us. Once we are aware of this it becomes a no-brainer. Why on earth would we create an unpleasant Earth by choosing to believe in something that is detrimental to humanity and the planet?

Some conditioned religious indoctrination belief systems based on fear, may also inhibit some people from discovering the benefits and power of Self Inquiry. For example, if someone has bought into a distorted version of religion where they decide to label something like self-inquiry as *"the devil"*, then out of their ignorance and fear, they will give themselves a reason not to explore it, like shooting themselves in the foot.

All of these potential resistances can also be dissolved with self inquiry, because all of their reasons belong to personality constructs which can be disintegrated and dissolved. If you are interested in truth, then you will gladly disintegrate and dissolve anything that stands in the way of knowing truth. But if you wish to cling to the lies of indoctrinated belief systems such as those found in some religions, then you will stay at that low level of evolution and ignorance until you are ready to go beyond them, because they all belong to the realm of thoughts, but deeper truth is beyond belief systems and the noise of the mind.

CHAPTER 14:

THE TRAP OF SELF-ESTEEM AND SELF-WORTH

"See I have no sense of self-esteem or self-worth, that's why any moment I'm willing to... if necessary next moment I'm willing to go, because I don't think this is worth anything, personally I don't think this is worth anything, keeping this on. But because it seems to be

> ***useful for many lives around us, we keep this going, but there is no self-worth because the sense of self itself is gone, so where is the worth? Self is not worth anything and that which is not worth anything, if you add esteem, that's lots of trouble."***
>
> \- Sadhguru

We have all often heard people in the mainstream system, influencers and mental health systems trained to preach to us about working on and investing more time and energy into our "self-esteem" and "self-worth", as though it's some kind of acceptable and permissible measurement to feeling ok and being mentally well enough, so that so called "professionals" can put a tick in their box. There have been entire programs and industry built on this mediocre understanding and idea, even mental health intake tests and questionnaires often ask about and focus on things like "self-esteem" and "self-worth", it's been a case of the blind leading the blind.

Don't get me wrong, some of these programs interpret "self" in a reasonably harmless way which can be beneficial, for example when they are about improving health and fitness.
However the idea of "self-esteem" and "self-worth" is a very mental concept attached to the false identity. It's what I call "Surface Dweller Perspective".
The Surface Dweller Perspective is the mainstream society's understanding of it which refers to the limited perspective of what people have been taught to believe and perceive "self" to be and what is believed and perceived to be a measurement of value and "worth" within the limitations of the conditioned mind. This ultimately results in a limitation of humanity.
Where value and worth has been obscured and placed in things that are arbitrary and fleeting.

So when this idea of "self-esteem" and "self-worth" has been applied to the masses who have been taught and conditioned to identify themselves with their false constructed ego sense of self. Then they are sorely mislead, blinded and led down a path of investing in and trying to improve their false identity construct sense of "self". Adding more "worth" and "esteem" to their personality construct measured only by what they have been taught to believe is "worthy" in comparison to the conditioned societies status quo, investing their time and energy into something which is ultimately a lie.

This then results in greater degrees of arrogance and also ignorance in the unawareness of not recognizing who they truly are, nor recognizing who others are. This is clearly seen after sufficient practice of self-inquiry where the false sense of self gives way to who we truly are.

CHAPTER 15:

ENLIGHTENMENT AND TRUE HAPPINESS

"You need nothing to be happy, you need something to be sad."
- Papaji

I will let you in on a little secret here now too, is that once you do this process of self inquiry enough, the process of the letting go of the heaviness of identity constructs, thoughts, beliefs and emotions, you can also become Enlightened.

This is true of any belief system including all religions, which only add extra weight and baggage to carry, I'm not saying that there is anything wrong with your belief systems if it serves you in some way to keep holding onto them or if you consciously use them to shape and create your reality, then by all means do that.

However, if you want to experience true enlightenment, then they are only additional weight that is carried which will only block you from experiencing true enlightenment. Because as I had previously mentioned, belief systems are like tools that we carry, when it comes to something like someone who adopts many religious belief systems, or any other indoctrinated belief systems and attaches them to their identity. Then it is the equivalent of being handed a bunch of tools and then dipping your hands into a bucket of super glue keeping yourself stuck to them, and then fooling yourself to think that they are you.

For many people, they have been heavily weighed down by all sorts of belief systems, like they are carrying the entire tool shed, most of them, they don't even realise they are carrying or realise that some are detrimental and really don't need to be carrying them.

In my own position I choose to keep my hands free, this way I can use any tool to shape and create my reality in any way that I need to. I can be a Muslim or a Christian or any other religion that I prefer to be at any given moment, I could even choose a combination, simply because I understand how the mind and reality works on a much deeper level. Because truth is not a belief system. When I look into such people, I can clearly see that they are just playing a character in the play, that they themselves are not even aware of.
To play such characters unconsciously for the long term is limitation, slavery to the mind and death of the life, while on the other hand, to

play such characters consciously as an actor that is not bound to them is freedom, unlimited, and the path to mastery.

When a *"me"* is held onto, it is a heaviness, a limitation holding us back from being able to change our costume and mask on the stage of life.

One cannot be fully enlightened while holding onto a sense of *"me"* because a *"me"* means that one is not operating from the God-self awareness of the "I" also known as the "I AM" consciousness.

Their dissolvement results in enlightenment because there is less and less to carry, making one lighter. That is why by dissolving it properly and letting it go, we are no longer weighed down by them and we are naturally relieved from those burdens to become enlightened. One can internally remove all reasons for not being enlightened. Thus in doing so; becomes enlightened.

Internally who is standing in the way of happiness? What is the reason that arises? What is the perceived obstacle and who does it belong to?

See that character that the thought belongs to, each time dissolving and disintegrating that character from within you because you are recognizing that its not you and doesn't need to be held onto any longer. It's no longer your baggage to carry because the truth is now revealed. This is what it means to become enlightened; when you are no longer carrying any of the baggage of your internal characters.
One could say that Enlightenment is one of the great beneficial side effects of Self-Inquiry.

THE END

FINAL THOUGHTS

I give gratitude and thanks to all those who have been supportive of my mission to heal and awaken all of humanity.

A special thanks to those who inspired and who guided me on my own path, both from earth and those from higher places.

A special thanks to Sadhguru for reviving the correct Yoga for the world, and for your ongoing wisdom and devotion for life and for awakening humanity.

A special thanks to Bhagavan Sri Ramana Maharshi for making self-inquiry more widely known and available to Humanity. The original documentation for the process of self-inquiry can be found for free in a multitude of languages at the website www.gururamana.org

This concludes the solution to suicide, however this is only the beginning of the series The Cure for Mental Illness, this is a major project which I have been working on for more than 10 years and there is still much more that I will be sharing with all of humanity.

Still to come, I will be revealing many things such as the many way's to oneness, the solution to racism, sexism and all other divisive projections. I will share my contact experience, my experience of death and return.

I will be bringing greater awareness and shining a light on the manipulation in education systems and various institutions, I will be discussing the mental health systems and how to cure diagnosed mental illnesses. I will be shining a light on the insanity of many social delusions and brainwashing agendas. I will also be teaching the so called "elite" who the true elite are, to not to be so ignorant and arrogant, allowing them the opportunity to grow and evolve too if they behave themselves. I will also be providing a guiding light for the future of all of humanity to reach it's highest natural potential. All of this to come and more.

If you want to support this mission, the best way is by following my social media and joining my mailing list at www.lightinthedarkness.online and you will be the first to know of any new updates.

Thank you.

www.ingramcontent.com/pod-product-compliance
Lightning Source LLC
Chambersburg PA
CBHW061738070526
44585CB00024B/2722